BUDDHA MEETS THE BEATLES
BUDDHA'S TOP 40 BEATLES' SONGS AND WHY

EDWARD SARKIS BALIAN

SSP

Silver Sky Publishing, USA
Silver Sky, Inc.
Encinitas, California
Farmington Hills, Michigan
760-809-9778

Revised Edition
Copyright © 2014 by Edward Sarkis Balian

Cover design by Dave Schindler
dave@design760.com

All rights reserved.
No part of this publication may be reproduced, stored in a retrieval system or otherwise copied in any manner without the expressed written permission of the copyright holder.

ISBN-13: 978-0-9831181-5-2
ISBN-10: 0983118159

Silver Sky Publishing, USA/Silver Sky, Inc.
San Diego, California
Farmington Hills, Michigan

www.BuddhaMeetsTheBeatles.com
760-809-9778

To Ray—

As written into his 1967 Cooley High School (Detroit) yearbook, "My dear friend since before *Ticket to Ride.*"

Producer, George Martin's early 1980's book, *All You Need is Ears*, U.K. version

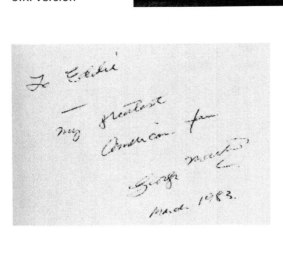

Producer, George Martin's personally signed book to the author, 1983, "To Eddie, my greatest American fan."

Acknowledgements

The author thanks the many people who have helped make this book possible. Thanks to Lynn Riccioni for editing and proofing of the text. Thanks also to the numerous panel members (you know who you are!) who made up our focus group team, evaluating the book concepts and cover designs. A huge thank you to Raymond George for his expert Beatles-related input, but moreover for his 50 years of friendship, knowledge, wisdom and inspiration.

For Silver Sky Publishing, USA, the crucially important "behind the scenes" industry research, marketing and promotion efforts were (and are) tirelessly and expertly supplied by Lia Beldin and Shannon Farrell. Legal assistance from David Moore (San Diego, California) and from my 30-year associate and friend, the late Michael Novak (Troy, Michigan), was also much appreciated. For her creative input, website design and overall marketing expertise, thanks are extended to the author's very talented and patient wife, Judith Balian, an important author in her own right.

As are all book efforts, Buddha Meets the Beatles has been "a long and winding road" indeed! It's difficult to sum up my gratitude on just one page of text, but I love you all, yeah, yeah, yeah!

Edwards Sarkis Balian
San Diego, California

Table of Contents

Preface	13
The Interview	24
5th Beatles?	104
Back Story	108
About the Author	111
Bibliography	113

Preface

What happens when two galactic icons meet up unexpectedly at a local radio station? Introducing Buddha Meets the Beatles!

Do You Like the Beatles, but Don't Know Much About Buddha?

If you are already into the Beatles, but know little about Buddhist philosophy, this book will offer new perspectives to the works of both. If you are just mildly curious about Buddhist philosophy, you'll find this book to be an easy to understand introduction to basic Buddhist principles, as explained, albeit strangely enough, through some of the Beatles' greatest works.

Are you an admirer of Buddha, but Don't Know Much About the Beatles?

If you are already familiar with Buddhist philosophy, you may be surprised by how the teachings of Buddha fit so seamlessly into his favorite Beatles' tunes and this may lead you to a deeper appreciation of the Beatles. As Buddha always said:

"When the student is ready, the teacher will appear."

Or in this case, Buddha might instead say:

"When the listener is ready, the Beatles' music will appear."

Recently, Buddha had occasion to drop in unannounced to the now famous DJ Eddie radio show at station KOMM, broadcasting out of La La Land, California, near San Diego. It was here, throughout an astounding on-air interview, that Buddha had an opportunity to critically discuss his favorite 40 Beatles' tunes from the group's official full portfolio of 216 songs. The outcome is entertaining, intriguing and not least of all, very enlightening. So here, taken directly from the on-air interview transcripts, Buddha delves into his favorite Beatles' songs and explains his attraction to each piece in both musical and spiritual detail. During the interview, Buddha will also consider the Beatles' group synergy on each recorded song and the lyrical "messages" contained in each of his favorite selections.

Intermingled with Buddha's synopsis, DJ Eddie, from his vast music and literary archives, will add Beatles' trivia facts and details surrounding each of Buddha's favorite tunes. The end result of this admittedly rather strange but powerful recipe is a book filled with Beatles' musicology coupled together with powerful Buddhist insights.

It all started one morning at our little radio station…

DJ Eddie: Good morning faithful listeners and welcome to another radio show from your fav host, DJ Eddie. I've got a great lineup of tunes for ya today here at KOMM radio, as I plan to get in ta' some ol' time rock n' roll. We'll be right back after this important commercial message from our sponsor.

(It is during this commercial break that DJ Eddie receives an intercom buzz from Rita, the radio station receptionist.)

Rita: There's some heavy-set dude out here wearing just a long orange robe and beat up sandals. I think he just walked in off the street. I don't even see a car out front. Poor guy looks penniless too. He says he's the Buddha visiting back here from the ancient-Eastern world and he would like to go on the air with you, if it wouldn't be too much trouble. Shall I give him a few bucks, call the cops, contact the homeless shelter or what?"

DJ Eddie: Buddha who? Is this some kind of "over my head, spiritual-genre" joke? Is it my son-in-law, Jay, playing practical jokes on me yet *again*?

Rita: He says his real name is Siddhartha Gautama, but everyone knows him worldwide as the Buddha and that we shouldn't be frightened. He says he is about 2,500 years old, but man, he sure doesn't look it! The guy also mumbled something about having compiled 40 of his favorite Beatles' tunes and now he wants to chat about them on the radio airwaves with you and our listeners.

DJ Eddie: Wha? How does he know about our station and my show?

Rita: He said he has a message for the world and his old pal, the Dalai Lama, had suggested that he drop in to your show. I guess this Lama guy is one of your regular listeners when he's in town, but it sounds like he travels a lot.

DJ Eddie: What is this Buddha guy doing right now?

Rita: Looks like he's sort of resting or something over on the sofa in our waiting area and he keeps repeating our radio station call letters, "omm…" Okay, so what in the heck do you want me to tell this poor old guy?

DJ Eddie: Poor old guy? Holy Batman, Rita, I think you're talking about the *real* Buddha right here in our studio. And, he's not "resting," he's *meditating* while he waits for us to decide what to do with him. I think this guy is the real deal. For God sakes, I don't know much about it, but Buddhist philosophy is named after him.

This isn't just big, this is *huge!* In fact, it could be the on-air radio event of all time. And, Rita, better do a Facebook post on this right *now!* Lock all the radio station doors. I want no interruptions and don't let him out of your sight. Send him into Studio A right away and I'll get an extra mike hooked up for him, then cancel out all upcoming scheduled commercial breaks.

Right here, right now, I'm going to interview this cool cat!

(Current commercial break ends)

DJ Eddie: Hey good folks, has DJ Eddie got a mega-surprise for you! We've got an ultra-special guest who just decided to drop by into our crazy show today. Talk about cosmic! Take ol' DJ Eddie's advice and tweet your friends and neighbors right now and tell them to tune in. I'm going to interview none other than the universe-renowned, Buddha, the great philosopher, and don't ask me why, but he wants to talk Beatles for our entire show! (DJ Eddie thinks to himself: "Wow, this is going to be the career radio show of a lifetime, with Nielsen ratings to boot!")

So, with no time to spare, let's get on with our interview. What are Buddha's insights into the Fab Four? Which specific tunes has Buddha chosen as his favorite Beatles' songs of all time and, most importantly, *why?* We should all enjoy this fascinating journey so fasten your seat belts.

(Buddha strolls into Studio A, sits down and Rita asks him about refreshments. Buddha requests green tea and crackers. Understandably, I need a drink of something a tad more powerful. We do a quick level-check on the mikes and start every audio and video recorder in the building, after all, this promises to be the radio interview of a lifetime!)

DJ Eddie: Buddha, Baby, thanks ol' pal for droppin' in. It's really great to see ya, but I've got to ask right off, why are you here? I mean, why my show? And, of all the things of heaven and earth, why do you want to discuss music and why the Beatles?

Buddha: First off, thanks so much for the welcoming hospitality. I know I just dropped in without invitation. As I mentioned earlier to your receptionist, I was recently speaking to my good friend, the Dalai Lama, about my great interest in the Beatles and my recent analysis of their music and he immediately suggested your radio station and with call letters like "K-OMM," how could I miss? In fact, in deep mediation in your lobby a few minutes ago, I was chanting some "om's" myself! I'm afraid your receptionist thought that I was a bit weird. If I frightened her, I'm so sorry.

DJ Eddie: Oh, that was our lovely Rita. She wasn't quite sure who you were or what this all had to do with my music radio show.

Buddha: Ah! There you have it all in a nutshell right off the bat. I'm here because of the exact reasons Rita just suggested.

DJ Eddie: Again, please?

Buddha: People the world over don't really know much about me, or my message, or exactly what I represent. Also, there's lots of misinformation about me and Buddhist thought. And, historically, my philosophy has many connections and parallels to the world of art, including music.

The kindness of you, Rita, and your radio station now give me the perfect avenue for communicating. And, how better to help me convey my philosophy of life than through the greatest pop-rock band in history, the Beatles? Indeed, it's a perfect match up all the way around. So here I sit. And, by the way, Sir Paul McCartney wrote quite a lovely song about a lovely Rita, but she was a meter maid instead of a receptionist!

DJ Eddie: *Lovely Rita,* uh? I can already see that you've got a knowledge of Beatles' music. But as a backdrop and before we get into a discussion of your favorite 40 Beatles' songs, our audience would love to start by knowing your opinions about each of the Beatles. For starters, you just mentioned Sir Paul McCartney.

Buddha: Sir Paul, indeed! His massive creativity never ceases to amaze me. Sir Paul McCartney has no limits. Paul keeps on creating new challenges for himself and then strives to attain them. His musical and creative boundaries, including painting, seem to know no end. Just when you think you have Sir Paul figured out, he surprises you with yet something even more creative, ambitious and entertaining. Where does all his creative energy end?

First, there is that singing voice of outstanding emotional range and quality. Then, consider his ear for vocal harmony, which is exemplary. While his melodic bass lines are stellar, his piano and guitar work is just as impressive. Paul's lyrics can be very touching, passionate and compassionate. On top of all that, did I mention that he is the most popular songwriter of the 20th century?

If that's not enough, his charity work has been praised worldwide and his children have never even shown up in the tabloids! I don't know what else I can say here other than Sir Paul McCartney is truly a living legend.

DJ Eddie: What words might you have for Paul?

Buddha: I think his never-ending creative projects underlie my thoughts: I never see what has been done. I only see what remains to be done.

DJ Eddie: Wow, you've certainly come prepared! And what about Paul's long time fellow composer, John Lennon?

Buddha: John was extremely enlightened and a true intellectual. But his life on this earth was full of success, disappointment, challenge, happiness, bitterness and suffering. Not surprisingly, John's creativity, imagery and lyrics were often full of insecurity, anger, tenderness, compassion and love, or all of the above at the same time.

Anyone who knew John would tell you that he was very temperamental, with chronic highs and lows. When he was depressed, he was very depressed. And when he was happy, he was very happy. Likewise, he could be incredibly bitter and angry with those around him or the world. He also could show great compassion and caring to a level as much or more so than anyone else you ever knew. There was always very little in-between with John, even among his closest friends and band mates. While at a new high point in his life with Yoko in New York City, his life was tragically taken from him. He lost his life and we lost a great artist and person. John's murder tells us: There has to be evil so that good can prove its purity above it.

As any Buddhist will attest, life is about suffering and the elimination of suffering. Through his senseless death, John's murder brought us suffering. Through John's worldly beliefs and lyrics, he still lives and he is still, in a way, trying to show us how to eliminate the suffering.

John's passion for the elimination of suffering started with each individual. He knew this and tried his very best, against numerous pressures, to use his fame for the advancement of peace and freedom on a worldwide scale. John will forever be remembered for both his music and his message. His vision of the world, as perhaps best communicated in his post-Beatles' song *Imagine*, was, and still is, shared by millions, including me.

DJ Eddie: If you could say one thing to John, what might it be?

Buddha: John fought for many causes and, at the same time, had many conflicts, public and private. I would advise him: To conquer oneself is a greater task than conquering others.

DJ Eddie: And George Harrison? He played the sitar so you must have liked him, yes?

Buddha: George was, and still is, very close to my heart, but it has little to do with his sitar.

For decades, seen as the "spiritual Beatle," George led the way for pop music to become a viable source of funding for charitable causes. This contribution was so big that it even transcended music itself. Case in point: *the Concert for Bangladesh*, held on August 1, 1971, in New York City, was beyond innovative at the time. While commonplace today, the whole concept of using pop music to raise huge amounts of money for charity was unheard of way back then. So be sure to credit George Harrison the next time you hear of a benefit concert being staged. But there is even more to George than his mega-giving to charities.

George was quite saddled artistically between John and Paul, but he handled it extremely well, which could not have been easy. Many of his musical contributions into the Beatles' songs were subtle but very significant. No small endeavor, George eventually broke away from the usual electric and acoustic guitars of Western music and introduced the Western world to Eastern music and, yes, the sitar, as you mentioned. As for his own compositions, it is no small wonder that I find many of his lyrics to be in direct alignment with Buddhist thought.

DJ Eddie: Any words for George?

Buddha: I don't think he would need too many words from me other than what he already knew:

You cannot travel the path until you have become the path yourself.

DJ Eddie: And how about the wildly popular Ringo? The young girls used to go completely nuts over him.

Buddha: While indeed quite popular among the young ladies, Ringo's important musical contributions to the group often go quite underrated. Musically, he added drums and percussion with an instinct all his own. His drumming style fits effortlessly into the group's sound. All very Zen, as we say in the Buddhist world. Whatever the song needed in percussion, Ringo had a knack for figuring it out and then executing it with precision. To the critical and careful Beatles' music listener, Ringo's contributions are clearly an integral part of the mix.

Last, but not least, in the most Buddhist of ways, he was a gentle, understanding peacemaker too; a personality that fit in beautifully with his other three band mates and the Buddhist philosophy.

DJ Eddie: And your words directly to Ringo?

Buddha: As a peacemaker, Ringo realized that friendship was the glue that held the band together, allowing the synergy to happen. To Ringo I would say: Chaos is inherent in all compounded things. Strive on with diligence.

Now, aren't you going to ask me about the "fifth Beatle?"

DJ Eddie: I'd love to, but I figured you might not know who I was talking about.

Buddha: Incorrect, my underestimating, musicological friend! There are numerous "fifth Beatles," but let me say that producer, George Martin, was perhaps the most unsung of all the many unsung heroes surrounding Beatles' lore. George Martin actually first signed the Beatles to a recording contract in 1962. His stellar legacy could have easily ended there, albeit significantly enough. But Martin did *far* more, as he was certainly the true "fifth Beatle" in the recording studio, helping them craft some of the greatest songs of all time.

In the most admirable examples of Buddhist thought, Martin initially sensed, then *cultivated* the positive energy and synergy he felt within the group. Part of the synergistic mix himself, Martin mentored the Beatles musically and became almost a father figure to them in the studio, providing both gentle guidance and profound wisdom in the making of hit records.

It was Martin, with the able assistance of first engineer, Geoff Emerick, who turned the four lads loose into an environment of nothing short of wild abandonment in studio creativity as "no" was never an option. *Any* idea was possible in George Martin's and the Beatles' musical world. This required Martin to bridge many gaps on numerous occasions.

For example, when London Philharmonic members were called in for Beatles' sessions, Martin had to write scores and conduct the players. And when the ultra-conservative "top brass" at EMI (later renamed Abbey Road) Studios had prying questions about the Beatles' expenses, studio time and commercial productivity, it was Martin mending the fences and bridging those gaps too. In short, through a combination of his formidable musical expertise and social finesse, Martin clearly recognized the genius of the Beatles, made it all somehow work and the rest just happened to become musical history. All very Zen, of course.

DJ Eddie: You've mentioned this "Zen" a couple of times now.

Buddha: I'm using "Zen" in a symbolic sense. In simplest terms, Zen is absolute purity. On a personal level, Abraham Maslow and other psychologists would call it "self-realization." Zen is the pure here and now and, through meditation, a mental state of Zen may be the closest we ever get to perfection.

DJ Eddie: So were the Beatles all Buddhists? Those early "mop-top" haircuts certainly were in contrast to having a shaved head like you! Buddha *(while scratching his very bald head)*: Well, you might think this sounds corny coming from me, but it kind of depends on your definitions, I guess. Watching the Beatles interact to create their art, they certainly demonstrated many Buddhist philosophical behaviors.

Like all of us on earth, their work was to discover their work and then, with their highest heart, give themselves to it. They did this through principles I call Right Livelihood and Right Effort, but more on that later. We were merely the beneficiaries by hearing their music.

DJ Eddie: Holy cats, what a beautiful way to put it.

Buddha: I specialize in beautiful.

Further, the Beatles were focused on creativity as an end in itself, not really fame or fortune. They wandered into largely unknown musical and even cerebral unknowns and took risks for the greater good. Certainly without debate, the cornerstone of their lyrics centered mainly around peace and love. And, of course, that too is deeply nested in my Buddhist philosophy.

Also, in answer to your question about haircuts or other behaviors, it's important for your audience to understand that following Buddhist philosophy in life does not necessarily mean that you are going to be…

- changing your name to Sunshine
- displaying a red dot on your forehead
- draping your doorways with colored beads
- having every other phrase in your conversations being, "far out"
- wearing flowers in your hair on weekdays
- burning incense called "Indian Sunset"
- standing on your head chanting "Om…"
- practicing Kung Fu
- having a gong in your living room
- being in a funny smelling, smoke-filled room
- sleeping on a bed of nails
- chanting in small groups at airports
- owning a wardrobe consisting only of 13 orange robes or
- shaving your head.

Regarding that final bullet point, wearing your hair a certain way has no bearing on practicing Buddhist philosophy in your life. But I'll get into a little more of all that later. Instead, let's get on to that fabulous Beatles' music.

DJ Eddie: Hey Buddha-Babe, let's start pullin' up Beatles' tunes from my archives of compact discs, iPods and classic vinyl 45rpm singles and long play albums. I'm so ready to rock. Let's see your playlist of top-40 favorite Beatles' tunes. I'm anxious to see your picks.

Buddha: I thought you would never ask! In preparation for your show, I put them all in chronological order, going by the original British release dates.

Buddha's Favorite Beatles' Songs

Chronologically by Album
(Parlaphone/EMI Original British Album Release Dates)

ERA I: 1963-1964

PLEASE, PLEASE ME (MARCH, 1963)
1. **I Saw Her Standing There**
2. **There's a Place**

WITH THE BEATLES (NOVEMBER, 1963)
3. **She Loves You**

A HARD DAY'S NIGHT (JULY, 1964)
4. **Can't Buy Me Love**
5. **Things We Said Today**
6. **I'll Be Back**

BEATLES FOR SALE (DECEMBER, 1964)
7. **I Feel Fine**
8. **I'll Follow the Sun**
9. **Eight Days a Week**

ERA II: 1965-1966

HELP! (AUGUST, 1965)
10. **Help!**
11. **The Word**

RUBBER SOUL (DECEMBER, 1965)
12. **We Can Work it Out**
13. **Nowhere Man**
14. **In My Life**
15. **Think for Yourself**

REVOLVER (AUGUST, 1966)
16. **Eleanor Rigby**
17. **Here, There and Everywhere**
18. **I'm Only Sleeping**
19. **Tomorrow Never Knows**

ERA III: 1967

SGT. PEPPERS' LONELY HEARTS CLUB BAND (JUNE, 1967)
20. **Strawberry Fields Forever***
21. **Penny Lane***
22. **She's Leaving Home**
23. **Within You, Without You**
24. **A Day in the Life**

MAGICAL MYSTERY TOUR (EP SET**, DECEMBER, 1967)
25. **All You Need is Love**
26. **The Inner Light***
27. **The Fool on the Hill**
28. **Hey Jude***

ERA IV: 1968-1970

THE BEATLES, A/K/A THE WHITE ALBUM (NOVEMBER, 1968)
29. **While My Guitar Gently Weeps**
30. **Dear Prudence**
31. **Bungalow Bill**
32. **Revolution***

LET IT BE (RECORDED IN 1968-69 BUT RELEASED MAY, 1970)
33. **The Long and Winding Road**
34. **Let It Be**
35. **I Me Mine**
36. **Get Back**

ABBEY ROAD (SEPTEMBER, 1969)
37. **Because**
38. **Across the Universe**
39. **Here Comes the Sun**
40. **Medley: Golden Slumbers-Carry That Weight-The End**

Notes:
*excluded from the actual Parlaphone/EMI album, instead released as a 45rpm single during the album's time period as indicated.

**extended play (EP) short set, not technically a Beatles' long-play (LP) album.

January, 1962, well before their invaision of America. Note Pete Best as drummer, far right

DJ Eddie: From the top, I should mention to everyone out there, that you might go ahead and look up these 40 Beatles' tunes on YouTube and play them along with me as we go through our radio interview. Fab! Example search on YouTube: I Saw Her Standing There Beatles

1: I Saw Her Standing There

Writing/arranging contributions as noted throughout the book:
(McCartney 70%, Lennon 20%, Harrison 10%)

DJ Eddie: I might not have guessed this first choice from you, *I Saw Her Standing There*, taken from the Beatles' very first album, *Please, Please Me*, released in March of 1964. Good a rock 'n' roll song as it is, it's just a silly little lyric about a teenage boy and girl at a high school dance. What could possibly be so deep and Buddhist about this?

Buddha: In less than three minutes the Beatles take you on a teenage thrill-ride. And speaking of rockin' positive energy within the group, there is also a powerful positive energy inside of Paul's lyrics. Young people could so relate to the song, as many a teenage boy or girl focused on their dream-mate at the high school dance.

DJ Eddie: But how could two teens checking each other out at a high school dance be related to Buddhist thought?

Buddha: Okay I'll grant you that at first listen, the words do seem silly and adolescent, but there is also a beauty to this simplicity and an optimism, attraction and fun element within. In fact, isn't this what life is really all about? I mean, I'm very often depicted as laughing, because life is so laughable. Many of us find joy and simplicity in our youth, but sadly tend to lose it later in life. As adults, don't we all take things a bit too seriously?

I relate to this song on a few different levels. The song showcases the early Beatles as a cohesive team, hard at work. Everyone in the group is singing or playing toward the greater good. A certain synergy is very prevalent on this cut, as would also be likewise demonstrated on numerous future Beatles' records.

So, in this song, there is a compactness, simplicity, teamwork and positive energy all present. You can actually hear it flow as one, if you listen closely. And all these fine attributes are basic tenets of Buddhist thinking and as such, are consistent with what I call the Eightfold Path, to be described later throughout our interview.

For now, just think about this: Happiness or sorrow, whatever befalls you, walk on untouched, unattached.

DJ Eddie: Walk where? Unattached to what? You're losing me…

Buddha: All on earth are walking a pathway, our journey through life, leading us ultimately to Nirvana.

DJ Eddie: Nirvana? Kinda like getting into the Rock 'n' Roll Hall of Fame?

Buddha: Better! In Nirvana, you are at one with the world. You have arrived at your perfection. You no longer need the world or anything in it.

DJ Eddie: And what of these "attachments" you speak of?

Buddha: Oh, more on that later.

For now, suffice it to say that those on earth seeking material or emotional "stuff" are attached to those things. And all of those things ultimately lead to suffering. As long as we are "attached" to worldly goods and emotions, we are still walking the path and our journey continues. The journey only ends at Nirvana.

Heavy stuff. For now, let's return to the music!

ABOUT THE MUSIC

DJ Eddie: With a superb rock-a-billy guitar break from George on his famed Gretsch Country Gentleman hollow-body electric guitar, this song booms out of the chute in a very early Beatles' session at the now famous Abbey Road studio in London. And Paul's rock 'n' roll vocal really rips it, starting right from his opening, *"One, two, three, FOUR…."*

This is just pure classic rock 'n' roll music, about as basic as it gets with its chord structure and arrangement. This is the "live" sound of the Beatles, almost as if they were on stage back at the Cavern on Matthews Street in Liverpool. The only problem with this song is that it ends!

THE TRIVIA

DJ Eddie: Paul's original opening line was *"She was just 17, a real beauty queen…"* Not too surprisingly, John hated that lyric and basically coerced Paul into instead using *"She was just 17, you know what I mean."*

Buddha: John was right.

Hey, cooperation and collaboration really *does* work! Peace throughout the world will only come through collaboration. I don't care if you're talking a rock 'n' roll band or the United Nations. And you can quote me on that, gang!

2: There's a Place
(Lennon 70%, McCartney 30%)

DJ Eddie: Here's another great song from the Beatles' first album in '63. But you mentioned the "Eightfold Path" a moment ago and you kinda lost me. What is this about anyway? It sounds mysterious and maybe even complicated.

Buddha: Not at all complicated my boy! Not at all. Not at all! There are eight very basic tenets of Buddhist thinking and philosophy. Simple as they may sound, follow them and your life will benefit greatly. I *guarantee* it. I'll be referring to many of these principles as we go through my favorite 40 Beatles' tunes for your listeners.

DJ Eddie: Hmmm. Okay, I think I get that, at least roughly. But golly, *There's a Place* is a pretty obscure Beatles' song. How do you figure this as one of your favorites and how in the world do "attachments" and your Eightfold Path fit into this?

Buddha: This is a lesser known Beatles' tune and is one of the earliest of original Beatles' compositions. Primarily written by John, he speaks of a "place," not unlike a sanctuary of sorts. While the lyrics seem rooted in the typical "teenage boy/girl" scenario, the images go well beyond and into a deeper sense of security and comfort.

In close parallel to John's lyric, Buddhist thinking is also centered on feelings of quiet inner peace and serenity. Two elements of the Eightfold Path, the principles of Right Mindfulness and Right Concentration are indirectly referenced here as needed routes to a secure and peaceful "place" that we all desperately want and need.

Right Mindfulness refers to being only in the present moment. Right Concentration means to stay highly focused in a calm mental and physical environment. To do these things the mind must be in the right, relaxed place.

DJ Eddie: Are you referring to a "place" more like a "sanctuary?"

Buddha: Yeah, we could easily draw that parallel.

ABOUT THE MUSIC

DJ Eddie: But there's even more here. As with so many Beatles' tunes, we again hear a fine example of team cooperation and collaboration. This is a very early example of John's harmonica playing, largely forgotten in the annals of Beatles' history. Also, listen for the somewhat raw, but nonetheless charming vocal harmonies between John and Paul.

Buddha: We could call the synergistic collaboration within the band an excellent example of the principle of what I call Right Effort, a third element of the Eightfold Path.

THE TRIVIA

DJ Eddie: *There's a Place* was so early and obscure in the Beatles' catalog, it wasn't much recognized, even during the wild 1964 "Beatlemania" period. Unknown to many, this song was released as a single in the U.S. on the meager Tollie Records label, in a previous contract deal coming well before top-shelf Capitol Records even wanted the Beatles. Yes, that Tollie record is quite rare and, in mint condition, is worth a small fortune today to 45rpm vinyl record collectors.

Buddha: Talk about positive productivity! The entire *Please, Please Me* album, from which this song was taken, was recorded in *one day* at the EMI studios, thus representing perhaps the most amazing 24-hour period in all of recorded music history!

DJ Eddie: Wow, I'm speechless over that.

Buddha: Then go with it: Say nothing unless you can improve on the silence around you.

3: **She Loves You**
(Lennon 45%, McCartney 45%, Harrison 10%)

DJ Eddie: Many of my radio show listeners sure know this tune as one of the most popular Beatles' songs of all, with the recurring *"yeah, yeah, yeah"* hook. A massive number one hit in early 1964 in the U.S., to put it mildly.

Buddha: I smile every single time I hear this tremendous early Beatles' anthem. The beauty in the lyric here is that a third-party comes into a break-up situation and promotes the pure, positive and simple value of the love between two people. Instead of coming from a high-pressure, aggressive love-triangle or similar perspective, this third-person only wants the two lovers to just reconcile and continue on. A fine example of Right Actions, Right Effort and Right Thought are contained in the storyline.

DJ Eddie: So these three Eightfold Path principles are tied to this tune?

Buddha: Yes, let me break it down for you. Right Action refers to everyday behaviors that promote peace and love. Right Effort refers to taking positive and harmonious actions to promote peace and love. Right Thought has to do with the positive spirit with which we approach everything. All three elements are woven into this song's message.

The song is upbeat, to say the least, infectiously catchy and extremely powerful, musically and sonically. It is both the point of view of the lyrics and the musical power being delivered that, in combination, are so captivating. My philosophy certainly sees love and its first cousin, reconciliation, as the basics for all good within the world. Rekindling of love is a good thing. To the two lovers, I say: To understand everything is to forgive everything.

DJ Eddie: What would you say to the guy who is delivering the message of this song to his friend?

Buddha: If he makes himself as good as he tells others to be, then he in truth can teach others.

By his intentions, he is using Right Thought. He shows Right Effort by applying energy toward the reconciliation of the lovers. He employs Right Action by taking steps to promote peace and love, so he doesn't just sit there and do nothing to correct the conflict.

ABOUT THE MUSIC

Buddha: As to the music, where do we start with this rock 'n' roll gem? The melody, vocal harmony, guitar chord structure, bass and drums (gee, what's left?) are all superb. In unique fashion, instead of starting with a verse, the song starts with the chorus, "*She loves you, yeah, yeah, yeah!*" This is very structurally unusual as songs go, but in this case, it's tremendously effective.

DJ Eddie: Holy cats! Man, I am totally freaked with your deep knowledge of this material.

Buddha: Dude, it's my job to go *deep* into everything.

John and Paul do the vocal leads while George's rhythm guitar work, echoing the "yeah-yeah-yeah" sung notes, creates a rock-solid "reinforcement hook" and backing. Paul's bass work is absolutely sensational, creating counter-melodies all its own. Ringo's drum work fits the song nicely. To conclude the tune, using George Harrison's idea of a G6 chord in three-part vocal harmony and also played on guitar, is downright brilliant and nothing less. All said, from start to finish, this is 2 minutes and 18 seconds of spectacular Beatlemania rock 'n' roll.

DJ Eddie: Did you watch the Beatles make their American debut on Ed Sullivan?

Buddha: Oh, Eddie, are you kidding? I wouldn't have missed it for the world!

When the Beatles performed *She Loves You* live on February 9, 1964 on the Ed Sullivan Show, to *grossly* understate it, they brought the house down!

This was one of the most important nights in pop music history. Want proof? If you, like me, were part of the 73 million who watched and listened on that Sunday evening so long ago, I'm *certain* you still remember that performance and where you were when you watched it. By the way, the 73 million viewers represented a whopping 38% of the entire U.S. population, including children and newborn babies! The FBI noted a significant decrease in crimes that night as even the crooks took the night off to watch the Beatles on TV.

Oh, by the way, a young boy named Phil Collins (later of rock group Genesis and famed solo career) and teenage pop singer Leslie Gore (hit songs: *It's My Party, You Don't Own Me, Maybe I Know*) were in the Sullivan live audience that night.

THE TRIVIA

DJ Eddie: *She Loves You* was another very early Beatles' recording that originally was found only due to an obscure, early deal on little-known Swan Records. This one record basically saved the Swan label from imminent collapse. Beatles' manager Brian Epstein agreed to release the song on Swan just for the exposure, as the Beatles still had no major U.S. record deal.

Well, as far as Epstein's attempt to gain exposure in the American market, this Swan deal *definitely* worked, to say the least as the Beatles became an overnight household name. *Yeah, yeah, yeah*, indeed! The Beatles made *practically no money* from this single, impossible as this may seem to believe today.

Buddha: Aw, money, who cares? Just an arbitrary currency largely used to purchase things we don't even need. And, as the old saying goes, you can't take it with ya and I've been gone and back enough times to know! But more on *that* later!

Rare, 3-inch diameter pin from 1964

4: Can't Buy Me Love
(McCartney 70%, Lennon 30%)

DJ Eddie: This song was highlighted in the Beatles' first movie, *A Hard Day's Night*, in 1964. Quite a nice segue from your song number three a moment ago, I think I get the thing about money and love, in that one can't get you the other. Is this why you like this song so much? Hey, I think I'm starting to maybe get this!

Buddha: Right on, DJ Eddie! This one really gets into my Buddhist philosophy. It could nearly become an anthem of sorts from the Beatles sung directly to the Western World.

The rain could turn to gold and still your thirst would not be satisfied.

So much of our planet, and particularly the Western hemisphere, is so saturated in materialism that people don't even realize they are living in the epicenter of it all. From Day One, we are indoctrinated with "buy this" and "buy that" so you can be a cooler person. From sexy clothing to white teeth, from overgrown SUVs to super-sized hamburgers to Beverly Hills mansions and on and on as the list is literally endless. Okay, so, what *can't* you buy? Love. As lead writer on this one, Paul hit the nail on the proverbial head. There is no fire like passion. There is no shark like hatred. There is no snake like folly. There is no torment like greed.

ABOUT THE MUSIC

DJ Eddie: And speaking of Paul hitting the nail on the head, this musical gem was yet another number one hit nailed down indeed. With its shuffle-style tempo, catchy hook, the usual great rhythm, bass and drum sections and hot vocals, this tune really delivers the rock n' roll goods.

Buddha: I can dig it. I mean, I *really* love it because the lyrics speak so directly to so much of the world's basic problem: materialism. As adolescent as the lyrics may sound, true peace throughout the world might really start to happen, if materialism and its corollary, greed, could just heed the simple sentiment within Paul's tune.

THE TRIVIA

DJ Eddie: *Can't Buy Me Love* was used as the musical backing piece to one of the best-remembered scenes in the boys' first film, *A Hard Day's Night*. In the scene, the four lads break away from their overwhelming Beatlemania pressures and backstage life by bursting out of a side door of the now, sadly demolished, Scala Theatre. The boys go frolicking nonsensically at the old Thornbury Road Playing Field.

Buddha: While Richard Lester's directing work is as brilliant and lively as ever, it is the *freedom* that the boys find in their "escape" that is the conceptual essence of this scene. As human beings, *freedom* is our natural state. We must all be free to choose our direction, free to make mistakes, free to reconcile, and free to move forward in life.

We must be free in order to break ourselves from life's suffering.

DJ Eddie: But you, the great Buddha, can help me, yes?

Buddha: I can offer suggestions and advice to those ready to hear about the path. But, in essence: No one saves us but ourselves. We ourselves must walk the path to enlightenment.

DJ Eddie: Heavy-osity, Brother!

Buddha: Dude, I don't deal with shallow! Do your listeners want a Madison Avenue soft soap job or do they want the truth?

5: Things We Said Today
(McCartney, 85%, Lennon 15%)

DJ Eddie: Buddha, you've chosen another fairly obscure album cut from a 1964 album, *A Hard Day's Night*.

Buddha: Yes, Eddie, I have. You know, whether a song was hugely popular or not, was never a parameter for me. I'm looking for messages. Many times a great message can be lost due to a low profile or lousy public relations.

DJ Eddie: What do *you* know about public relations? I mean, I'm the one here in the entertainment business!

Buddha: You don't have to be in radio or TV to see the value of public relations. Relating to the public is extremely important. In fact, it's downright essential, even in the spirituality business. I'm here on a publicity campaign right now. People need to know what I'm *really* all about, not just guess about what they think Buddhist philosophy is about.

DJ Eddie: Oh yeah, I guess I see your point. "Power through knowledge," as my old high school teacher used to say?

Buddha: Ah, you've hit on the Eightfold Path principle of Right Understanding or the ability to see things as they really are, not how you would like them to be. This is an essential part of my philosophy. A person needs to *truly* understand, not just *think* they understand.

But back to the song message. Moody and melancholy Paul speaks of introspection and gratitude for the important things in life. As he looks back on a relationship, he holds a quiet thanks for all the feeling he will hold for his lover, at the time, Jane Asher, to be someday gone. He also makes a point of recognizing how valuable and rare a sincere love can be.

The lyric also reflects upon how love is all-powerful, whether two people are actually together or not. In love, the spiritual bond goes on perpetually. This is a profoundly beautiful concept in keeping with my Buddhist philosophy.

ABOUT THE MUSIC

Buddha: As to the music, this haunting tune is mainly constructed around a striking acoustic guitar rhythm track, using a unique, double-time strum. The bridge (i.e., "….*me? I'm just the lucky kind*….") is another measure of musical beauty. The vocal harmony of Paul and John are worked out brilliantly, as usual.

THE TRIVIA

DJ Eddie: In a quite unusual personal message for Paul, his lyric is a sort of swan song for his long time relationship with Jane Asher, sister of Peter Asher, of Peter & Gordon fame. Paul of course wrote smash hits for the 1960's P&G duo, including *World Without Love*, number one in the U.S. in April 1964, and *Woman*, number 14 in the U.S. in January 1966. Another P&G classic, I Go to Pieces, number nine in the U.S. in December 1964 is also often credited to Paul but, for once, he did *not* write it, as that tune was penned instead by Del Shannon, known for his own smash hits of *Runaway* and *Hats Off to Larry*.

It should also be noted here that Shannon performed and released the *very first* Lennon-McCartney composition into the U.S. market in 1962, *From Me to You*, and it went practically *nowhere* on the charts! One year later, for the Lennon and McCartney writing team, it would be a far different story.

Buddha: You bring up two important names. Del Shannon passed years ago by suicide. From our highly limited earthly perspective, yes, it is proven yet again that life is full of suffering, but Del is destined to come back again and again to continue to work through the suffering, as we all will, until we finally get it all figured out.

I might also add here that Peter Asher currently lives in Los Angeles and is still playing and producing music. He was also very involved in raising money in the charity campaign for the seriously injured Mike Smith, brilliant lead singer and keyboardist of the Dave Clark Five (hits *Glad All Over, Bits and Pieces, Because, Over and Over* and many others). The highly talented Smith passed a few years later, but he too is still alive and well back in the cosmos, as we all will be. Death is just a rebirth and our cycles continue until we work it all out. Yes, all *very* Buddhist, but what the heck else did you expect from me?

DJ Eddie: Okay, now just wait a second. You are getting pretty far out with this "coming back" jazz. When a person croaks, aren't they just plain ol' dead with a capital "D," you know, the Big Bye-Bye, as it were?

Buddha: Actually, it's even *more* far out to think that this little life is all there is and then "poof," all of a sudden you are totally gone forever. I find that thinking quite demeaning to a deceased human being. The human spirit is far more valuable and powerful than that.

Actually, upon death, you are gone only in the way people knew you, on this earth, in this momentary here and now. But in the infinite or cosmic sense, upon death you are simply recycled or repurposed, if you will. Post-death, you just keep coming back for another shot at enlightenment. You keep dying and returning inside our cosmos until you reach that ultimate state I call Nirvana.

But until you reach Nirvana, the suffering goes on, in one form or another, until you figure it out. This happens at the ultimate point I call Right Knowledge.

DJ Eddie: Ouch! I wish you would stop bringing up suffering.

Buddha: My philosophy is about *eliminating* suffering, 100 percent. Sound good? It is.

You know, I didn't want to bring it up earlier, but on a completely unrelated subject, I've noticed that since we started this interview, there have been no commercial breaks. How come?

DJ Eddie: Oh, I told Rita to cancel all the commercials so I could just concentrate on interviewing you.

Buddha: Oh, nonsense! I'll tell you what, let me do a few commercial breaks for your station's and the listeners' benefit? How about it?

DJ Eddie: Sure. I'm so pleased with our interview so far, why not? And my ratings are going through the roof! Rita says the office phones been ringing ever since you came on and a crowd has been forming outside the studio as well. Heck, why not give you some commercial air time? But you're not going to try to sell us religion or something are you?

Buddha: I'm not selling a thing for money. Simply put, I am just trying to convey my perspective on the real meaning of life. Your listeners can take it or leave it. They are free to choose any path they wish. I'm a huge believer in personal freedom, you know.

DJ Eddie: Folks, so we're going to our first commercial break of the show, brought to you by the Buddha himself. I'll be right back after this from Buddha.

Commercial Break

Buddha: Greetings listeners of KOMM. Yeah, this is the Buddha speaking coming to you from the DJ Eddie radio show.

Tired of your everyday hum-drum life? Looking for exciting new products and services? Time to shift gears in your life? Looking for love in all the wrong places? For once, would you want things that really deliver as promised?

Well, my Buddhist Do-Wop line of spirituality is far from new and it's not even improved. In fact, my stuff is so ancient it makes TV reruns of *Leave it to Beaver* seem like first season, 1957, pilot episodes. My product is not mega or ultra or plus. And there's no light or diet version either.

So, if you've tried the rest now try the best: inner peace! But *wait,* there's more: order now and receive everything you need for free. Note that this offer is good for only the first three billion residents of Planet Earth, so there's no real hurry either. Actually, the truth is when you are ready, I will appear so feel free to look me up anytime. Now back to our KOMM radio show with your host, DJ Eddie.

Vintage print ad for the "fiddle bass" by Hofner.

6: I'll Be Back
(Lennon 80%, McCartney 20%)

DJ Eddie: Hi fans, we've returned from our break and we're ready to spin more tunes here at KOMM. We're goin' back to July of '64 with this cut from John Lennon. Buddha, say what to this one?

Buddha: Resiliency and devotion to your inner beliefs and drive are signs of strength of character. It's always so easy instead to just give up on your heart's hopes and dreams. In this sleeper tune among all the Beatles' classics, John clearly speaks of a tenacity based around a potentially lost love.

Importantly, John finds fault only within himself, not in his lover or anyone else. It is *he* who has been humbled and who has consequently learned some important lessons. This thinking demonstrates a level of inner wisdom not reached by many in life. This is clearly the basic element of Right Thought in action.

DJ Eddie: It is a haunting melody indeed, but definitely not dance music for my wild, Saturday night shows. The tune is from the *A Hard Day's Night* album of July 1964. To this day, very few people are even aware of this song. As might have been said on Dick Clark's American Bandstand TV show, you can't dance to it. Where's the beat, man?

Buddha: But the beat that really counts is the one in your heart.

ABOUT THE MUSIC

Buddha: Dance music, no, but written around a haunting minor key, John's song creates a deeply moody emotion. While there's certainly a place for "wild party, dance music," as you call it, much of life's deeply profound beauty is found in quieter, more intimate moments.

As exemplified by the three part vocal harmony by John, Paul and George, this song demonstrates an exquisite beauty all its own.

THE TRIVIA

DJ Eddie: The chord structure of *I'll Be Back* was evolved by John from an earlier U.S. hit single written and performed by previously mentioned, Michigan's Del Shannon, who had toured with the Beatles in their very early years. As we have seen, Shannon crops up more than once in Beatles' history.

7: I Feel Fine
(80% Lennon, 15% McCartney, 5% Harrison)

DJ Eddie: Hey, KOMM listeners out there, now *this* track moves! When I no sooner start spinnin' this platter, the kids get to dancin.' Baby, let's rock out! A number one hit in 1965, this was a superb tune.

Buddha: Yeah, and speaking of superb, what is more superb than the love between two people? Combine this with the innocence and optimism of two *young* people and you've got not just one of the most powerful moments in life, but also some of the most delicate, intricate and beautiful moments in life.

DJ Eddie: And add to that, rock 'n' roll! *Yeah, baby!*

Buddha: As John Lennon so accurately relates in this driving electric guitar rocker, he's flying high on his new found love. As you listen to this song, you can almost feel him floating on a cloud, high above the hum-drum of boring, everyday life. This guy, at this moment, is really both high on life *and* in love. That's grand energy!

ABOUT THE MUSIC

Buddha: In a hard-driving electric lead guitar, played by John (surprise: not George!), on his Epiphone Casino electric hollow body, the overall sound of this record exemplifies the mood as very "up" and positive. It's *impossible* to listen to this song and not get happy and laugh. And you know: I'm always laughing, because the world is so laughable.

THE TRIVIA

DJ Eddie: *I Feel Fine* begins with a bizarre amplifier sound effect on the open, electric guitar note of low E. John discovered this "feedback" note quite accidently while rehearsing the song in the studio. He loved the electronic sound which was generated by simply leaning his Gibson acoustic-electric guitar against his amplifier.

Buddha: Lennon's feedback effect used here was years before Jimi Hendrix and was probably the first such effect ever appearing on a record as an intentional part of the song. As we came to expect later, the Beatles were full of innovation and John's intro to *I Feel Fine*, in a way, hinted as to the future of their vast musical creativity to yet come. My elements of Right Thought, Right Actions, Right Concentration are all at play here.

8: I'll Follow the Sun
(McCartney 85%, Lennon 10%, Harrison 5%)

DJ Eddie: And now listeners, here's number eight on Buddha's Hot-40. This tune is from the *Beatles for Sale* album of December '64. The tune was never released as a 45rpm single, but still a fairly popular album track at the time.

Buddha: Our audience might be surprised to hear that this song's lyric represents what was pretty much my own attitude when I left my wife, son and huge palace to go out into the world in order to seek Truth and try to find the key to relieve all of life's suffering.

DJ Eddie: *You* left your wife? I never thought of you as a "love 'em and leave 'em" sort of a guy.

Buddha: Well, there was a far greater good involved. I left my hotsee-totsee royal palace for a life of poverty in order to better understand the world. I eventually returned to my family as my sojourn ended. In my travels, I learned that the world was perpetually in a state of suffering, and I eventually worked out a way to conquer it.

DJ Eddie: Suffering, again, you say? You've brought that word up a lot.

Buddha: I can't bring it up enough. *Suffering*, and better put in the positive sense, the *elimination* of suffering in life is truly what my philosophy is all about. As I said earlier, eliminate all suffering and you attain Nirvana, that special place of ultimate and everlasting enlightenment.

And, as *I'll Follow the Sun* implies, following the sun is not only romantic, but it is also an ambitious mission and is deeply spiritual. The path of the sun is characterized by warmth, not cold. It speaks of positive vision, not negative. It is optimistic, not pessimistic. The sun is bright and life-giving. If there is any better physical entity in the skies above for us to follow, I do not know of it.

We will all pass away, like a sunset. But knowing we will be back, like a sunrise, how can we quarrel? Follow the way of virtue. Follow the way joyfully through the world and beyond.

ABOUT THE MUSIC

Buddha: Basically a simple folk song composed and sung by Paul, this tune has a beautifully sweet melody. George supplies the equally fitting, simple guitar lead during the instrumental break. It is a very clean production and recording, but with a profound message.

THE TRIVIA

DJ Eddie: Paul says that Buddy Holly's song writing was a major influence on him for this composition. While Paul's lyrics speak of abandoning an innocent, significant other, "sometimes you just have to do what you have to do," as Paul later explained it publicly.

Moreover, was this song a cloaked, private message foretelling the future of Paul's eventual break-up with long-time lady-friend Jane Asher? We'll never know. We *do* know it is a beautiful song.

Buddha: Ah yes, beauty is everywhere, in everything, and as conveyed in this song, even if it is nested in the bittersweet.

Adding vocal tracks at Abbey Road

9: Eight Days a Week
(Lennon 45%, McCartney 45%, Harrison 10%)

DJ Eddie: From December '64 and the *Beatles for Sale* album, this tune was released as a 45rpm single here in the States. It's number nine on Buddha's chronological list. So what gives with *"eight days a week?"* It sounds silly.

Buddha: How much love is enough in this world? John Lennon and the rest of the Beatles seem to have the answer here: The limits of love exceed all possible, worldly constraints of time and space, as eight days in a week exceeds the possible.

From the Buddhist perspective, the lyrical idea here far exceeds the simple concept of an attraction between a boy and girl. Interpreting the lyric in a far wider meaning, an overabundance of love is only more of a good thing. There is no downside to loving to one's full capacity or even to *beyond* one's apparent full capacity. Following the philosophy rooted in these lyrics, one is well on their way along my Eightfold Path indeed.

It might be time to mention that, at the risk of oversimplification, the Beatles answer to all this was encapsulated into one over-riding word: *love*.

The light of one candle is never diminished by the lighting of other candles from it. Likewise, love is never diminished by being shared.

ABOUT THE MUSIC

DJ Eddie: George's superb use of his newly acquired Rickenbacker 12-string electric hollow-body guitar fades *in* as the intro of this song in a very tuneful and ear-grabbing way. Fading in the electric guitar was bizarre enough and coupled with an all new electric 12-string sound was a totally creative, fresh sound that caught the ear of nearly all musicians at the time.

George seemed to have a real knack for using this instrument and other future stringed instruments to follow over the years, in very captivating, creative and infectious ways that *always* seemed to brilliantly fit the songs. Interestingly, the song ends as it starts with the same chord progression.

THE TRIVIA

DJ Eddie: John maintained that this song was originally written by Paul to be the title track of their second movie, originally titled, "*Eight Arms to Hold You,*" the movie later released as *Help!* In fact, the movie's original "*Eight Arms….*" title appears just under the song title printed on the USA- issued 45rpm single.

The phrase "eight days a week" was coined by Ringo, who was well-known for such idiosyncratic expressions over the years, including "it's been a hard day's night" and "tomorrow never knows," both other famous Beatles' song titles.

George's Rickenbacker 12-string made famous on numerous Beatles' recordings. Hear it used predominately on songs, If I Needed Someone, Eight Days a Week and A Hard Day's Night. This specific guitar even launched an entire band: the Byrds!

10: Help!
(Lennon 90%, McCartney 10%)

DJ Eddie: The title of your song number 10 is also the namesake of the Beatles' second movie. In fact, the song itself opens the movie and was released as a 45rpm single to great success in August of 1965. Tell us about your take on *Help!*

Buddha: Is it a sign of weakness when we call for help? In the Western world, it often is taken as such. But the real truth is that everyone, yes, *everyone*, needs support and understanding at some time in their life. Even if you are one of the most famous and financially successful people on earth, like Beatle, John Lennon, for instance, there will always be instances when you need outside assistance, and sometimes even need it desperately. To appreciate this best, one must have Right Understanding.

As John himself discussed publicly many times, he was feeling very overly needy when he wrote this song as the pressures of being a world icon were getting to him. Our lesson? Is fame and fortune in life the grand accomplishment that many of us think it is?

DJ Eddie: But isn't asking or crying for help seen as such a weak thing to do?

Buddha: Only the unenlightened feel that way, I'm afraid. In times of great stress or challenge in life, no one is above asking for help. Through the centuries, I've been around to see some of the world's most so-called "powerful" people cry for help.

DJ Eddie: So getting help from others is the key?

Buddha: Others can eventually help you see yourself. But you are the key to you.

Look within. Be still.

The whole secret of existence is to have no fear. Never fear what will become of you, depend on no one. Only the moment you reject all help are you freed.

ABOUT THE MUSIC

DJ Eddie: Serving as the title track to their second full length movie, *Help!* contained an extremely interesting vocal treatment as John supplied the lead voice while Paul and George added an intricate and very creative background lyric "preview" of John's lead lyrical lines to follow. Somehow the syncopation works beautifully, as usual with the Fab Four!

Buddha: It's great fun to watch our boys on camera bouncing along, singing and silver screen, you really feel like you are right in there standing on stage moments too, and this was one of them.

THE TRIVIA

DJ Eddie: MTV and VH-1 eat your heart out! If you want to see some very early and very cool "music videos," you need to specifically watch the musical segments in this movie. While *A Hard Day's Night* won far more critical acclaim in motion picture circles, it is in *Help!* Beatles' performances really shine, lip-synced no matter!

And with that folks, it's now time for another quick commercial break from your friend and mine, the Buddha.

COMMERCIAL BREAK

Buddha: Hi again friends and Beatles' fans worldwide. Are you always feeling tired? For that quick 3PM pick me up, put down that caffeine and try my special no-cost formula instead: weather permitting, just go sit under a tree for a few minutes and *do nothing*. Listen, smell, observe. Relax. It's "serenity time."

This "do nothing" commercial was brought to you by the tranquil cosmic forces of Nirvana. We hope to see you there soon.

Now back to KOMM as our radio interview continues with DJ Eddie.

11: The Word
(Lennon 90%, McCartney 10%)

DJ Eddie: We're back. Up next on Buddha's Beatles' list is number 11, *The Word*. It's a rather unknown album track from 1965. So, Buddha, what's up with this one?

Buddha: John Lennon sums it all up pretty much right here and right now when he says that love is not only *his* answer, but *everyone's* answer. John sees love everywhere and in everything. This is a very cosmic approach and nothing comes closer to Buddhist philosophy.

There is pleasure and there is bliss. Forego the first to possess the second.

While not recognized as one of the Beatles' more famous or popular songs, this obscure album cut, from the LP, *Rubber Soul*, strikes a solid chord with me. Of their entire music portfolio, I can't think of any better Beatles' lyric that epitomizes the Buddhist philosophy. Oh, if only the world would *just take* John's advice.

However many words you read, however many you speak, what good will they do you if you do not act upon them?

ABOUT THE MUSIC

DJ Eddie: This song is musically notable on two distinct counts. First, the strange high harmonies by John and Paul were rarely ever used either before or after this peculiar recording. Second, a strange off-beat continues throughout the song, as supplied by a repeating and somewhat dissonant guitar chord and this all coupled with John's great lyrics. The song has an overall "un-Beatles" kind of sound to it, but somehow, as usual for the Fab Four, it works out brilliantly.

Buddha: In a way, this song marks the true starting point for the Beatles' future promotions of "love" as beyond a simple, partnership romance and instead, a concept of worldly application. In Beatle-talk the song lyrics represent, "one small step for love, but one giant leap for lovekind," as astronaut, Neil Armstrong, might have put it.

THE TRIVIA

DJ Eddie: In his famous interview for *Playboy* magazine published in January 1981, John said that *The Word* was about the "love and peace thing." Instead of just singing about boy loves girl, this song represents a transition of sorts, as it is one of the first Beatles' songs to go to a higher place regarding the power and value of love.

Buddha: I'm with you 100 percent, Eddie, but I'm not sure *Playboy* magazine would have been the venue I would have chosen to explain it! But, hey, whatever works in this interference-filled, carnal environment.

Whatever words we utter should be chosen with care for people will hear them and be influenced by them.

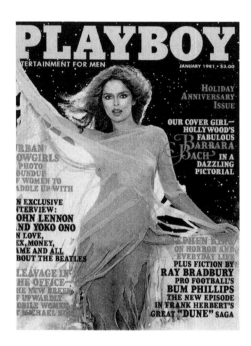

January, 1981

12: We Can Work It Out
(McCartney 50%, Lennon 30%, Harrison 20%)

DJ Eddie: Ah, this is one of my personal favorites. It was a 45rpm single from late 1965. A real masterpiece, yes?

Buddha: This song represents yet another fine collaboration between Paul, John and George. In fact, it should be noted that the Beatles did not always work together as a cohesive unit, as revisionist history often falsely recollects. The truth is that their close collaborations existed on only a very few songs and *We Can Work It Out* was one of them. A real gem!

Working things out necessitates at least six of my Eightfold Path principles: Right Understanding, Right Thought, Right Action, Right Effort, Right Mindfulness and Right Concentration.

As mentioned before, any self-respecting Buddhist can tell you that life is full of suffering and challenges. In this song, we *clearly* hear both the 'ying' and the 'yang' of it.

DJ Eddie: Ying and Yang? I've heard of 'em! Weren't they the group that opened for Cheech and Chong in the late 1970s?

Buddha: No, silly boy, ying and yang are the two opposing and equal forces as found throughout the universe, keeping everything in perfect harmony and balance.

Paul's lyrics talk optimistically of working out the miscommunications, while John's "middle eight" section, as musicians call it, warns that *"Life is very short and there's no time for fussing and fighting, my friend."* So there you have it, offered most succinctly. There are two equal and opposite ways of evaluating everything, including relationships. And we continually seek solutions. Yes, all very Buddhist, indeed.

DJ Eddie: Gee, I've played this song a million times but never thought of it *that* way.

Buddha: Start.

DJ Eddie: Yeah, I think I can dig it.

Buddha: *Dig It* was another John song from a much later album. (Buddha winks)

ABOUT THE MUSIC

Buddha: As mentioned, the wonderful collaboration of Paul, John and George is pulled off brilliantly on this all-time Beatles' classic. Paul had the original idea for the tune, while John added the middle-eight lyrics section ("*Life is very short....*") and also added a superb harmonium track comprised of thick, backing chords. The sound of the harmonium stands out instantly and somehow fits the song beautifully.

Meanwhile, George is credited with the idea of a quite drastic, waltz time change of tempo for John's middle-eight section. The overall result of this entire mixture: a magnificent song that lives on as a true Beatles' classic.

THE TRIVIA

DJ Eddie: *We Can Work It Out* was recorded about the same time, October 1965, as Lennon's pet song at the time, *Day Tripper*. Lennon had always wanted *Day Tripper* to be the "A-side," or preferred side, of a two-sided vinyl record. As it turned out, both songs appeared together for the new platter and both were considered huge hits.

The Beatles carefully spent 11 hours crafting and recording *We Can Work It Out*, a song of just over three minutes duration and it did turn out to be the "A-side" after all, as radio station DJ's and the general public seemed to gravitate to this side of the vinyl "45." That said, *Day Tripper*, for its part as the B-side, is to this day also considered a top-notch rocker.

Buddha: Ha! A-sides, B-sides, vinyl records, platters, cassettes, CDs, iPods, iTunes and blah, blah, blah. In the great vastness of the cosmos, no one really cares about the medium that delivers it. When it's great art like this, it's just the art that matters, not the technicalities.

So, in that vein, don't even bother worrying or caring one second about me. It's only my *message* that counts.

13: Nowhere Man
(Lennon 80%, McCartney 10%, Harrison 10%)

DJ Eddie: My old rock band in Detroit covered this tune back in '68, but I never thought I'd be interviewing Buddha about it! *Nowhere Man* was a hit 45rpm single released in the States in 1965.

Buddha: In our world, it is very easy to become disenchanted and lose our way. We can feel helpless, powerless and lost. Admittedly, singing about himself, John Lennon was there. But also offered up in the lyric is the idea of hope and new direction.

Optimism prevails! So, yes, there is an answer. But what John did not mention is that you've got to seek the right answers to the right *questions.*

Your worst enemy cannot harm you as much as your own unguarded thoughts.

DJ Eddie: In John's case, it sounds like Beatlemania was closing in on him, yes? He was stressed out, I guess.

Buddha: Just like our ol' Elvis Presley. Could *any* mortal absorb this level of adulation and keep his mind clear?

If a man going down into a river and is carried away by the current, how can he help others across?

ABOUT THE MUSIC

Buddha: On the recording, John applies a double-tracked lead vocal. George's lead guitar tone is ultra-bright, an effect they never used again on any Beatles' song. There is also a most curious single chime note added at the conclusion of the center section of George's guitar solo. Paul's high harmony vocal on the last measure of the lyric adds a unique, very characteristic and classy "Beatles'-ending" to the song.

THE TRIVIA

DJ Eddie: *Nowhere Man* was part of the live set for the Beatles' final touring performance at Candlestick Park, San Francisco, California, in August of 1966. Also, the recording of this song at Abbey Road Studios (then EMI) apparently drove their engineer, Norman Smith, later of Pink Floyd fame, and Beatles' producer, George Martin, to near insanity as the Beatles' quest for "more treble and high end" on the lead guitar challenged all the technical limits of the studio.

Buddha: As most serious artists, the Beatles pushed hard for what they wanted and stayed incredibly persistent until they got it. These guys were not into compromising within their art.

And, so it is also, with chasing perfection on earth. To get to Nirvana, one must stay extremely persistent no matter what the external pressures of daily life. There are no shortcuts. It takes hard work and great tenacity. I might add: Easy to do things can be harmful to oneself. Exceedingly difficult things to do are things that are good and beneficial. Life is challenge, yeah, yeah, yeah.

John's Epiphone Casino hollow-bodied electric guitar used in many Beatles' recordings starting about 1966, but perhaps made most famous in the group's final "roof-top concert" at Apple in London.

14: **In My Life**
(Lennon 80%, McCartney 15%, George Martin, 5%)

DJ Eddie: One of the Beatles' most famous songs yet but it was never released as a single. Buddha, please tell our listeners your view of it. *This* ought to be good, folks!

Buddha: Yes, this truly is one of John Lennon's best loved, most remembered and widely covered compositions and for good reason. What is life but a series of experiences and events all strung together?

There are only two mistakes one can make along the road to truth: not going all the way or not starting.

In this song, John is describing his journey along life's path. While all in the present, as places, things and people interact with us, it is only the memories of the moments, all strung together, that give us a feeling of a continuous life. And what does the sum of these life places, things and people really mean? According to John, the bottom line is: "*I've loved them all*" and I, the Buddha, can't improve on that.

The way is not in the sky. The way is in the heart.

DJ Eddie: Yeah, I don't know much about Buddhist philosophy other than what you have been telling us, but in this song, everything you've just said makes sense. Coolness!

Buddha: Coolness, indeed. John said publicly, many times, that this song was his "first serious composition." Yoko Ono has mentioned that many fragments of the lyrics appeared very early on in John's "master notepad," which she still possesses. Ka-boom! I'd like to spend a few years looking through *that* journal!

The song lyrics were originally derived from the childhood locations John recalled and revisited around Liverpool, most notably in the areas of the docks, rail yards and Penny Lane. Later, John mixed in memories of his friends and most particularly, yet another "fifth Beatle," Stu Sutcliff, who unexpectedly and tragically died years earlier of a brain hemorrhage. Yes, still more suffering in life. But like all others who have passed, Stu never really left and is back somewhere in the cosmos working it out toward Nirvana like the rest of us.

DJ Eddie: There you go with the "suffering" bit again! You are becoming a pain in my derriere with this negativity!

Buddha: Life's pain is a given. It is your suffering that is optional.

You can't ignore suffering any more than you can ignore death or life. As I've said, suffering is all around us, I'm afraid. But so is the repeating cycle of life and death as we reincarnate. And that's very beautiful. I'll tell you once more and keep telling you until you get it: I'm about eliminating suffering. Dude, I'm on *your* side.

ABOUT THE MUSIC

DJ Eddie: And speaking of beauty, let's not forget about the beautiful melody and musical performance of *In My Life*.

The basic musical "hook" is a simple multi-note melody played off a D guitar chord. There is also some mild disagreement about Paul's involvement, or not, with the melody. Note the double-speed piano solo by Beatles' producer, George Martin, giving a very classical-sounding harpsichord effect.

Although this song has been covered by many artists, the Beatles-Lennon version is relatively simple and straightforward, production-wise. As we both mentioned earlier, today the recording shines through as one of the most beloved of John's compositions.

Buddha: By now, even the Beatles' doubters were seeing that these guys were not just a mop-topped, teenager-based, hysterical fad. The musical evolution and revolution of the Beatles was now clearly in motion.

THE TRIVIA

DJ Eddie: This is one of the very few Beatles' songs that are quite controversial in terms of composition. Both John and Paul had different recollections of exactly how the song was written and, to compound things, both Beatles were inconsistent over time as stated in their later interviews on the matter.

Moreover, there appears to be at least a few points of certainty: John wrote all the lyrics, while Paul wrote a portion of the music, while producer George Martin played the piano solo. Exactly how much of the song's *entire* melody was written by John seems debatable and, at this point in time, we'll probably never know for sure.

Buddha: I'm glad you brought this up and it's an interesting mystery all right. But neither you nor your listeners are supposed to know *everything* in life. If you truly want the answer to this question, you'll have to get to Nirvana to find out. Of course, *I* know, but I'm not tellin.'

15: Think for Yourself
(Harrison 80%, McCartney 15%, Lennon 5%)

Buddha: Listeners, you will recall that one of my critical Eightfold Path elements is Right Action. This includes the negative behaviors of cheating and lying. Beatle George takes on the latter full-on in this, one of his earliest compositions.

DJ Eddie: I remember earlier seeing Right Action in your Eightfold Path, but can you be more specific about what it means, in a practical sense?

Buddha: The mind is everything. What you think, you become. Think for yourself, indeed! Simply put, you can lie. You can aspire to having material things at all costs. And you can put a lot of energy into these things, but you're going to be on your own. I won't be there to help you. Right Action, Right Speech and Right Mindfulness are all elements of the Eightfold Path. In other words: take positive action, don't lie, and stay in the present.

DJ Eddie: But what makes the Eightfold Path and its elements so essential anyway?

Buddha: There are no shortcuts to the ultimate goal, Nirvana. The *only* way to it is the Eightfold Path. For example, Right Action and Right Mindfulness are but two of the eight elements that help us get to the final, eighth step. And, it is only at that final culmination of the eight steps, Right Knowledge, that you have eliminated suffering and attained true enlightenment. That is Nirvana. There are *no* shortcuts and numerous detours along the way. Get it?

DJ Eddie: Listeners, guys and gals, are you with me? It all sort of adds up to a *"groovy kind of love"* as Wayne Fontana and the Mindbenders may have put it. Yeah, I think I actually *am* getting it!

ABOUT THE MUSIC

DJ Eddie: Regarding the song itself, while one of George's first set of philosophical lyrics, the musical elements of this song also break some new ground. Most notably, Paul's bass playing here was quite innovative at the time, utilizing a second, double-tracked, bass part with heavy, distorted "fuzz" tone, in addition to a normal bass track. Listen very closely and you will hear both bass tracks.

Paul got this creative bass idea largely from famed producer, Phil Spector, who had been experimenting with the technique. In later years, bands everywhere started using, and over-using, fuzz tone on everything, from piano, to guitar, to bass and even on vocals. For better or worse, Paul gets the credit.

THE TRIVIA

Buddha: When asked about exactly *who* this song's biting and stern lyrics were directed towards, George commented that he really wasn't sure, but he thought it was probably aimed at the UK government bureaucrats! Okay, so after hearing all of George's lyrics in *Think for Yourself* should we laugh or cry? There seems to be a painful truthfulness in here somewhere.

Right Thought? Right Action? Right Speech? Right Effort? Right Mindfulness? Right Concentration? Right Knowledge? Hmm...according to my report card, and George's, it seems like your world governments are flunking on all counts.

DJ Eddie: Well, it's time for another quick commercial word from our guest, Buddha. We'll be right back with the show as our Beatles extravaganza continues.

Commercial Break

Buddha: Road trip coming your way? Boston? New York? San Diego? Portland? Get the vehicle that takes your life to a new and exciting state and without the use of any fossil fuels. Try a totally new way of travel: *relaxation!* You'll be glad you did! And when you get to that state of total relaxation, just tell 'em, " Buddha sent ya."

George's renowned Gretsch Country Gentleman, largely designed by guitarist legend, Chet Atkins. Watch George play it very skillfully on February 9, 1964 on the Ed Sullivan Show! (Note that Harrison devotees have often recognized his guitar work on this first Sullivan performance as particularly outstanding.)

16: Eleanor Rigby
(McCartney, 100%)

DJ Eddie: Hey listeners, we're back from commercial and here's Buddha's number 16, a Beatles' hit single from '66 and for many of us in radio-land, this was a very classical sounding piece for our pop audience at the time. Was pop music going Mozart or what? Were the Beatles abandoning their legions of fans, their enormous financial success and even rock 'n' roll? The people in our entertainment industry were going bonkers trying to figure it all out!

Buddha: This song easily made my list of favorites. The lyric by Paul is a brilliant commentary on how the common people within the world are so easily overlooked, generally ignored, pushed aside and ultimately, quickly forgotten. All of that behavior is not to be admired or even condoned. Each and every single thing in the cosmos needs its recognition and respect, including all of the Eleanor Rigbys in our world.

That said, ol' Eleanor may already have been way ahead of other mortals as she perhaps already understood more than we know. In that light, you may have been feeling sorry for someone who was already way ahead of you.

Make an island of yourself, make yourself your refuge. Make truth your island, make truth your refuge. There is no other refuge.

DJ Eddie: So what do you want *me* to do? Should I feel sorry for all the Eleanors on earth or not? I mean, should I drop a dime or a $20 bill into the Salvation Army red kettle at Christmas time? Aren't we all are just stuck here on this goofy planet anyway?

Buddha: First off, yes, you *are* stuck, quite stuck in fact, on this goofy planet. Second, I don't want you to do anything you don't feel you want to do. You are here in this life to live it as you see fit. Third, my philosophy is not a book of dogmatic rules or a sales pitch. And fourth, you will keep returning to our cosmos via reincarnation until you finally get it right. So there.

DJ Eddie: Whew…I'm sorry I asked.

Buddha: Behaving properly in daily life is easier said than done, of course. The principles of my Eightfold Path are simple enough to write out, but not so easy to follow.

DJ Eddie: Okay, so what *do* I do?

Buddha: I say, start simple. For instance, the very next time you encounter a lonely person like our Eleanor, instead of with sympathy or pity, treat them with openness, compassion, empathy, respect and goodwill. Your Right Actions will come back to you a million fold. As Nike says, *just do it.*

ABOUT THE MUSIC

DJ Eddie: Buddha, what do you make of that crazy string section playing on this song? I thought this was supposed to be rock 'n' roll! Were the Beatles trying to pull a fast one on us?

Buddha: This is a masterpiece of music, by any genre label you want to pin on it. *Eleanor Rigby* represents the perfect combination of writer Paul McCartney and producer George Martin, while both together arguably at one of their many simultaneous artistic pinnacles.

Paul's lyrics are profound, the melody is gorgeous, the vocal and string harmonies are understated yet complementary, glorious and most befitting the song. George Martin's scoring for the string quartet is particularly superb. Throw in audio engineer, Geoff Emerick's, "tight miking" technique to produce that "in your face" biting string sound and you've got historic Beatles' magic yet again.

DJ Eddie: Listeners, if you should ever question the raw beauty of this melody, listen to a simple piano rendition. While the chord changes are very simple, C to E-minor, the melody is haunting and overwhelmingly gorgeous.

Buddha: Simple is always beautiful.

THE TRIVIA

DJ Eddie: On Stanley Street, just around the corner from Matthews Street and the Cavern, is an interesting sculpture of the fictitious Eleanor Rigby done by Tommy Steele.

Or was she so fictitious?

In the mid-1980s a gravestone marked "Eleanor Rigby" was found at St. Peter's Woolton, the spot where John first met Paul, no less. According to the grave, the actual Eleanor Rigby was born in 1895 and passed in 1939 at age 44. For his part as composer, Paul claimed no prior knowledge of this grave marker. *Eerie!*

Buddha: Not so eerie from how I see it. Life is full of internal cross-connections, but we often have blind spots so we must be spiritually "plugged in" to pick up on all the cosmic connections that present themselves in our daily lives.

17: Here, There and Everywhere
(McCartney 90%, Lennon 5%, Harrison 5%)

DJ Eddie: From the sophisticated and highly regarded *Revolver* album of 1966 comes another track of total Beatles' coolness. All I remember is that every girl I ever dated loved this song.

Buddha: Well, I am just so pleased to hear of your former love life successes, but more seriously, love *really is* "here, there and everywhere." In fact, it is this level of full awareness of love that ultimately leads us through the Eightfold Path and into Nirvana. Not only the love from another human being, as shared in the song lyric, but love as appreciated from *all* sources, *truly* here, there and everywhere. Love the people, the animals, the plants, the rocks, the sea, the wind, the sky and even that goofy guy who cut you off in traffic this morning. Love every molecule in the entire cosmos. Become one with the world and you will *arrive*.

DJ Eddie: Go Daddy, Go! Buddha, Baby, this sounds so cool all right and it seems so easy.

Buddha: You are correct and incorrect at the same time: it *is* very cool, but it also *is not* so easy. It is all the distraction in the world that runs interference at us and it is *that* which makes it so tough. Most people have trouble separating the daily street noise from the really important elements of life, like love.

You say, "Go, Daddy Go?" Well, yes, but where are *you* going?

With goodwill for the entire cosmos, cultivate a limitless heart: above, below and all around.

DJ Eddie: But isn't love all around us already? It's in a million poems, song lyrics and even in the diamond ring TV commercials at Christmas time!

Buddha: Much of this "love" is quite dramatic, but superficial. And often, the love is merely innocent, or not so innocent, infatuation. Or, in some cases, is it really lust that is being promoted and commercialized?

Love, in the universal and honest sense as is written in *Here, There and Everywhere,* is very different. It is not about shallow emotions and lyrics about the moon, the sun and the stars. It is not about having sex with someone until they displease you, then calling it quits. It is about understanding a far deeper meaning of love, and moreover, loving the entire universe.

ABOUT THE MUSIC

Buddha: Oh, this is yet another great Beatles' tune, this one with many cover versions done of it over the years. Most notably, check out Celine Dion's version. Wow, even George Martin was totally bowled over by Celine and he should know, as he produced *both* her and the Beatles' versions!

DJ Eddie: In the Beatles' version, written by Paul and sung by him in his falsetto voice, his vocal self-harmonies are very delicate and his melody is one of the Beatles' and Paul's, best yet to this release date. There is some interesting guitar work here as well, supplied by John and George. Paul holds down a very tasteful bass line too. In total, the song is instantly likeable and easily rates as another true Beatles' classic.

THE TRIVIA

DJ Eddie: Paul wrote *Here, There and Everywhere* while sitting over at John's house one afternoon. He was attempting a musical "answer" of sorts to Brian Wilson's recently released *Pet Sounds* album by the Beach Boys.

Most Beatles' scholars agree that the song was no doubt directed toward Paul's long time lady-friend, Jane Asher, the sister of Peter Asher of the group Peter & Gordon, as noted earlier.

Buddha: Oh, and speaking of Brian Wilson, there's another musical genius. Hey, DJ Eddie, want to do another radio interview sometime about *his* music? *God Only Knows*, I'd love to do it, yeah, yeah, yeah!

Rickenbacker 4001S bass used by Paul starting in 1967 and used heavily throughout his later recording and touring career with Wings.

18: I'm Only Sleeping
(Lennon 85%, Harrison 10%, McCartney 5%)

DJ Eddie: Buddha, you've chosen another fairly obscure track from the *Revolver* album. Why such an apparent interest in these sleepy lyrics?

Buddha: Sleep and relaxation are stepping stones to true meditation. And meditation is one of the cornerstones of Buddhist philosophy. The ability to relax your mind and focus is central to maintaining positive thoughts and actions. More formally, in the Eightfold Path, this is again what can be referred to as Right Thought, Right Concentration and Right Mindfulness, all three elements integral components of the Eightfold Path.

DJ Eddie: Yo! You are blowing my mind again. But I must admit that as my listeners and I are learning more about the Path and its ingredients, it's beginning to make more sense all the time. But I'm not seeing the connection to this song.

Buddha: Patience, my DJ friend, patience.

What I like in *I'm Only Sleeping* are John's lyrics of total abandonment of stress or tension. As he completely relaxes at his home in Weybridge, he drifts away from his life's attachments, worries and concerns. It's an escape, but a positive escape, as he is *"taking my time"* and watching *"life going by my window."* It is only a very short walk down the road from here to formal meditation and then onward to the purity of Zen.

DJ Eddie: So the song sort of gets you on the right road toward Nirvana?

Buddha: Yeah, I guess you could say that. Try thinking of the lyrics as a sort of roadmap helping you relax so as to avoid detours and distractions as you drive down the Path.

By your own efforts, waken yourself, watch yourself. And live joyfully. You are the master. Be still.

ABOUT THE MUSIC

Buddha: This is a most interesting production, as the music tends to exactly fit the mood of the lyrics, very slow and dreamlike. First off, Paul's bass work, particularly in the stop sections of the song, are almost lullaby-like with his slow, sluggish playing. Most fittingly, it sounds like he's half-asleep himself.

But moreover, it is George's superb lead guitar work that helps separate this song from other Beatles' tunes of that era. The guitar solos are recorded in a normal manner, but then were laid in backwards while mixing down the master recording. But in order to make this all work, the guitar notes had to be written and played in the correct backwards sequence in the first place. Get it? Very tricky and very ingenious, indeed.

So what you end up with are all the correct notes fitting the song and chords going forward, but the guitar sound itself is all backwards. Notice how all of George's lead guitar notes fade *in* instead of fade out, as would be normal for picked guitar notes.

DJ Eddie: The Beatles weren't known much for "normal," I guess. But they sure were innovative and creative.

Buddha: "Normal" and "genius" tend not to go together much. Why is so-called normality so coveted anyway? If our world today is so normal, how come we are in such a mess? We need less normal and more extraordinary.

THE TRIVIA

Buddha: In March of 1966, when John penned this song, journalist, Maureen Cleave, commented that he was "probably the laziest person in England." In that same interview by Cleave, John said, "we are (as the Beatles) more popular than Jesus now. I don't know which will go first, rock 'n' roll or Christianity."

Of course this quote was immediately taken out of context as John never meant to compare the Beatles to Jesus in any sort of self-glorifying way.

Instead, he meant that if the Beatles or rock 'n' roll were, in fact, more popular than Christianity, then that was not such a good thing for society.

DJ Eddie: How did you feel about the Cleave story at the time it came out? I know kids were burning Beatles' records in bonfires, especially in the Bible Belt south. There was a lot of outrage goin' down.

Buddha: John's actual message was very genuine and profound. He also went through a lot of that word again: *suffering*, as a result of the story as it appeared in the press. This entire episode, from the muckraking point of view, really ticked me off.

To John, I could only say: Just as a solid rock is not shaken by the storm, even so, the wise are not affected by praise or blame.

19: Tomorrow Never Knows

(Lennon 90%, McCartney 10%)

DJ Eddie: Buddha-Buddy, you've got me floored with this pick, the last song on side two of the *Revolver* album. What in the heck is going on with this choice? The song sounds very bizarre and even unmusical at times. Is it even considered a "song," per se?

Buddha: The lyrics are from the ancient *Tibetan Book of the Dead* and this Buddhist volume is considered the bible of Tibetan Buddhism. The book is a classic.

The concept is that of the "void" and reaching it is what John was attempting to say in this song. John's vocal, with its strange effects, applied by producer George Martin, gave John his desired sound of "a choir of monks singing high upon a mountaintop."

As the lyrics say, *"Turn off your mind, relax and float downstream...."*

DJ Eddie: Okay, okay, I'm floating, I'm floating. But where am I *going*?

Buddha: Your journey involves your elimination of suffering via the Eightfold Path. You get there through meditation and the purity of Zen, by relaxing and floating downstream, as John Lennon might say. Right Knowledge or Nirvana is your ultimate destination.

DJ Eddie: Man, that's a heavy travel schedule. What about my frequent flyer miles?

Buddha: Oh, you'll get your mileage bonus all right, but redeemable only when you get to your final stop. So fasten your seat belt and hang in there, Daddy-O!

ABOUT THE MUSIC

DJ Eddie: As alluded to earlier, this song is filled with strangeness. As mentioned, John's lead vocal is accomplished by multi-tracking his voice, which is also run through a Leslie speaker, originally designed for organ. It is this special unit, with its own tube-driven amp, that also powers a rotating speaker in the base of the cabinet that creates the whirling, twirling sound in his vocal.

For its time (1966), this was outrageously creative. Producer, Martin and engineer, Geoff Emerick, again deserve special recognition for pulling this all off within the strict confines of the ultra-conservative EMI studio.

In addition, Paul's contribution to this song is adding tape loops made by him on his personal Grundig tape recorder. Paul experimented heavily and eventually discovered that his laughing greatly speeded-up and played backwards on an endless tape loop gave a most unique effect, sounding to me a bit like a chorus of cats crying out for milk, "mew, mew, mew." At any rate, these sound effects most beautifully fit the song, another common trademark found throughout many of their works.

THE TRIVIA

DJ Eddie: There are slight differences between the mono and stereo mixes of *Tomorrow Never Knows*. The stereo version, now much more commonly heard, has a slightly different ending with more prevalent piano and John's vocal, at one point, contains significant microphone feedback. These elements are completely absent from the mono mix, although the vocal tracks are the same takes and are obviously identical. Go figure.

Buddha: Things are not always what they seem. Case-in-point: most believe *Tomorrow Never Knows* was the last song recorded for the *Revolver* album, but it was actually the first. This must have set quite a tone for the album's later sessions.

From the listeners' point of view, *Tomorrow Never Knows,* as the final cut on the *Revolver* LP, served as a telling signal of what direction was next to come from the Beatles: *Sgt. Peppers' Lonely Hearts Club Band* was soon to make music history.

20: **Strawberry Fields Forever**

(Lennon 90%, McCartney 5%, Starr 5%)

DJ Eddie: Buddha's next pick is from very late 1966 and it's another pretty far out tune. Remind me not to ask you to bring these records to my next DJ dance gig, okay?

So what attracts you to this one, Buddha?

Buddha: "Strawberry Field" (no "s") was John's special place for quiet meditation and escape. Only a five-minute walk from his childhood home on Menlove Avenue in Liverpool, it was at this nearly sacred spot that John could fantasize, relax and dream. Maybe even meditate. It is here, above most or all other places in his world, that he could exercise Right Concentration, Right Thought and Right Effort.

DJ Eddie: Holy blazes, it sounds like John's lyrics hit on no less than *three* of the Eightfold Path principles in just one song.

ABOUT THE MUSIC

Buddha: And just listen to the result. This is a fantastically beautiful and haunting ballad, with passionate lyrics, while overflowing with avant-garde musical creativity all mixed in.

DJ Eddie: Yikes! A real mind-blower!

Musically, there is so much more going here it is hard to know where to start. Originally, as a slow blues number, John's song morphed into a surreal set of images and lyrics and, somewhere along the way, changed tempo and key. After two distinct takes in the studio, John favored parts of both takes, but neither take in its entirety.

Enter producer, Martin. At John's request, Martin sped up part of one take and slowed down part of the other take then, with scissors and adhesive tape in hand, combined the two pieces of recording tape physically into the song we hear today! The song of *Strawberry Fields*, as we hear it today from start to finish, never has actually existed live!

The ending of this song is particularly noteworthy and is extremely avant-garde for its time, or even for today! In a combination of forward and backward music and backward lyrics, the song fades out with an almost carnival atmosphere. This certainly was no standard dance tune! At this stage, from late 1966 to early 1967, the Beatles were doing nothing less than redefining pop music.

THE TRIVIA

DJ Eddie: A few remaining photos of the original Strawberry Field show a very cool Victorian building which served as the neighborhood Salvation Army orphanage. The grounds were filled with huge trees. Sadly, the building was torn down years ago and replaced with a modern block structure. But, through Lennon's artistry of music and lyrics, the Strawberry Field imagery will live on truly *forever*.

Buddha: Forever is a profound concept. Yeah, I'm into it in the most positive way, as in *forever enlightened*.

DJ Eddie: Man, I hadn't noticed the time as we're up for another quick commercial break from Buddha. Listeners, we'll be right back.

Commercial Break

Buddha: Friends, are you carrying an outdated smartphone?

Fhorgitt abowt it!!!!! You're all ultimately heading to where your smartphone will seem like a total moron. So laugh it up like me, the Buddha. Send in any four yogurt lids in care of this station and get your free Wisdom- Pac, containing my hyper-cosmic laughter dust. No cost, no obligation. No bead-laden salesman will call.

I guarantee that I can make you laugh at the world.

Vintage print ad for John's Gibson J160E (far right); used extensively throughout his Beatle years.

21: Penny Lane
(McCartney 85%, Lennon 15%)

DJ Eddie: Hi listeners, we're back.

Hey Buddha, ya know I visited Liverpool back in 2007 and I drove right past Penny Lane. It looked just like a little roundabout bus stop sort of place and nothing very special really. But what's your take on it, Big Daddy?

Buddha: Paul's whole idea here is to take a nostalgic look back at childhood innocence and it works beautifully. Using Right Concentration, Paul creates a very sharp and focused positive image. Note the carefully crafted words that not only give us an image of the roundabout known as Penny Lane but, in effect, a precise, well-focused motion picture of a series of events taking place there. As you listen to this song, you can't help but get drawn into Paul's "movie" yourself.

DJ Eddie: You speak of Right Concentration quite a bit so will you elaborate?

Buddha: Sure, Eddie, glad to. Right Concentration is all about sharp focus. Think of a camera lens viewing life. While the lens can frame a scene, the image doesn't make any sense until all the objects within the frame are correctly focused. In life, you can "frame" a situation, but can you clearly see all the meaning within it?

All too often in our lives, we see the general images, but our focus is not sharp enough to give us all the information that is there. We falsely think we are seeing "the whole picture," but we are only seeing the vague images and not the full story underlying everything in the frame. Right Concentration or the ability to focus helps us better understand everything we encounter.

To that end, Right Concentration brings us the sharp focus we need to help us through the Eightfold Path and on to you know where: our ultimate destination, Nirvana!

DJ Eddie: So Paul's lyrics supply the sharp focus to bring us *Penny Lane?*

Buddha: Well, yes, in a manner of speaking. Through sharp focus, Paul helps us understand *Penny Lane* on a deeper level. As you listen to the song carefully, you actually begin to *feel* like you are there. It's no longer just about a generic bank, a fire truck or a rain storm. Through sharper focus, *Penny Lane* feels like a real place.

ABOUT THE MUSIC

DJ Eddie: Regarding the music, together with the Beatles' playing and George Martin on piano, quite a corps of musicians were brought in on this recording. Of particular note, Paul's bass playing is a standout on this cut so just listen for his rich bass line riffs throughout the song.

Buddha: Eddie, let me add that *Penny Lane* is generally regarded to be entirely Paul's composition so one may be a bit surprised to see John Lennon listed as a contributor. In fact, going back to John's *In My Life*, a reference to the Penny Lane roundabout was written by John, but later removed from the final recording take.

John's *Strawberry Fields Forever* also represented a journey back into earlier thoughts, feelings and recollections. Thus, childhood images and fantasies had already started being explored by John before Paul began to compose *Penny Lane*. John also contributed the last full verse of lyrics for the song. It is also interesting to recognize that while John helped Paul compose, Paul also helped John. One case in point among many: Paul's very creative effects added to John's *Tomorrow Never Knows*, as discussed earlier. Teamwork lives!

THE TRIVIA

DJ Eddie: As mentioned earlier, having personally visited Penny Lane, it is indeed fascinating to see such an average looking place in reality take on such an air of artistry and significance. Penny Lane is nothing more than a simple little suburban roundabout with a center bus stop and a few little surrounding shops. The rest is Paul's loving recollection and imagination. Buddha's points earlier about Right Concentration and focus are very well taken as it is to Paul's credit that Penny Lane takes on any significance at all.

It is worth mentioning here that there are two versions of this song, each with different endings. A "3pm" version as it is known has an ending piccolo trumpet solo. This earlier piccolo trumpet ending solo version was used largely as the promotional 45rpm record for radio DJ's. The officially released version of the song had this ending solo removed.

Interestingly, both John's *Strawberry Fields Forever* and Paul's *Penny Lane* ended up on the same Capitol 45rpm single (#P-5810, 1967), arguably perhaps one of the most creative and artistic pop records of all time. Both tunes were to appear on *Sgt. Peppers' Lonely Hearts Club Band*, but unfortunately were cut from the album. Can you imagine the staggering overall quality of the already iconic *Peppers'* LP if these two spectacular songs had been properly added to this album?

22: She's Leaving Home
(McCartney 90%, Lennon 10%)

DJ Eddie: Yet another tune from your list that has a very classical flavor to it. *She's Leaving Home* was an album cut from side one of *Sgt. Peppers' Lonely Hearts Club Band*.

Buddha: This song tells of the all too common story of parents giving everything but love to their children. Well-meaning parents so often confuse the giving of material things as a substitute for love and, of course, it is not.

In Buddhist philosophy, a form of "attachment" comes about from a focus on wants and desires, including material things. These attachments lead only to mankind's eternal suffering. This line of thinking is best summarized in what I call the Four Noble Truths:

1) Life is suffering,
2) Suffering is caused by attachments,
3) Eliminate your attachments and you will eliminate your suffering and,
4) Follow and practice the Eightfold Path as it is the only way to eliminate your attachments and future suffering.

So, in *She's Leaving Home*, we have materialism confused with love, all encapsulated in a touching song by Paul. The father says that he "*gave her everything money could buy*," while the mother reflects that "*our baby is gone*," and so the suffering continues.

DJ Eddie: Kinda sad, man…

Buddha: No, Eddie, *very* sad. Lots of suffering. We can look at the suffering from both the child's and the parents' points of view, to which I say: Look not to the faults of others, nor to their omissions. But rather look to your own acts, to what you have done and left undone.

ABOUT THE MUSIC

Paul came up with this musical idea very suddenly. So suddenly, in fact, that when he wanted to rush into the studio to lay down the tracks, producer Martin, wasn't available as he had a session already booked for singer, Cilla Black.

In an impatient and nearly inexplicable move, Paul instead hired Mike Leander to orchestrate the piece. Leander's work was quite impressive as the string treatment is masterfully executed. One can only speculate as to what Martin could have done with the song. Having been the "5th Beatle" since the early days of Beatlemania, Martin was understandably offended and moreover puzzled by Paul's impatience.

On the vocal tracks, in the form of a "call and answer" to Paul's lead, John adds great backing vocals throughout the song, "...*we gave her everything money could buy, buy-bye.*" John's haunting voice fits the mood.

Even though never released as a 45rpm single, *She's Leaving Home* is another all-time classic. It proves yet again that the four lads from Liverpool were far more than a rock 'n' roll band, as they continually pushed the boundaries of pop music again and again. And the Beatles were far from musically or culturally finished!

THE TRIVIA

DJ Eddie: On February 27, 1967, Paul read an article in London's *Daily Mail*, describing that a young runaway girl, Melanie Coe, had abandoned her car and vanished. Her parents were distraught and perplexed. Paul wrote the song very quickly using only the information available in the news story and he had absolutely no idea of who Ms. Coe was.

Now it gets really interesting. When the Beatles had first played on the British TV show, *Ready, Steady, Go!* back in October 1963, none other than Ms. Coe was on the set as a dancer, both during rehearsals and the actual airing. If this strange coincidence were not enough, she had won a mime competition on the show and none other than Paul McCartney presented her with an award. Amazingly, all of this a full four years before *She's Leaving Home* was ever written.

Buddha: As I mentioned earlier, life is full of these cross-connections, if we are open enough in our consciousness to see them. This kind of thing has happened to Paul more than once.

23: Within You, Without You
(Harrison 100%)

DJ Eddie: Your song number 23 from your list is again not an immediately recognizable Beatles' tune. This one from the *Sgt. Peppers'* album was never a single but clearly was George Harrison's major contribution to the album. Your thoughts?

Buddha: There is perhaps no other Beatles' song that comes closer to my spirituality than this one. George's message here is that we are all one, as a single cosmos. We are, in fact, all very small and just part of a system that encompasses all which surrounds us.

We are what we think. All that we are arises with our thoughts. With our thoughts, we make the world.

DJ Eddie: Daddy-O, this sounds heavy…

Buddha: It is. The basic theme in this lyric is that the ever-elusive peace of mind each of us seem to strive for can only be found within yourself and you can only get there by seeing the *whole* picture. I mentioned this earlier in regard to Right Concentration or focus. If you wanted to begin on the

Eightfold Path leading to inner peace, George's lyrics in this song just might be your starting point.

In essence, peace comes from within. Do not seek it without.

ABOUT THE MUSIC

DJ Eddie: The song is almost totally a George Harrison effort and his fingerprints are all over it in both words and music. In fact, none of the other Beatles were even present during most of the sessions. When Paul, John and producer Martin first heard a rough demo session of *Within You, Without You* they weren't much impressed and, more likely, didn't quite know exactly what to make of it. After all, the song is rooted in Eastern music and is from basically another realm outside of our Western music scale. The piece has no Western music chords per se and carries an extremely unusual time signature, or beat.

Buddha: Suffice it to say that on *Dick Clark's American Bandstand*, "Make It or Break It" segment in the 1950's, this song would have garnered a "you can't dance to it" reaction from teenagers!

Yet for all its Eastern musical strangeness, *Within You, Without You* seems to fit beautifully onto the *Sgt. Pepper's* album. In the 1967 "Summer of Love," the song contributed a backdrop anthem of sorts and adds multi-musical dimensions to this already iconic and colorful album.

DJ Eddie: And what about that strange laughing at the very end as the song fades out?

Buddha: Oh, that. The multi-tracked laughing at the fade-out ending of the song was provided by Harrison himself. I might dare say that this was an acknowledgement toward me, the Buddha. You know, I'm almost always depicted as laughing. That's me, always laughing at the world, and for jolly good reason: the world is often a comic mess, yeah, yeah, yeah.

THE TRIVIA

Buddha: Coming from the East, I really dig this track! To record the piece, George brought in many of his Eastern musician pals and their acquaintances. And Beatles' right-hand man, Neil Aspinall, plays tambouras, a strange Eastern percussion instrument. Producer Martin did have a heck of a time writing a score for violin and cello to go with the Indian instrument ensemble, but, as usual, he came through brilliantly, adding an even more mystical sound color to the recording.

A fashion tie. *Everything* was Pepperland in the "Summer of Love," 1967!

24: A Day In the Life
(Lennon 75%, McCartney 25%)

DJ Eddie: You follow your number 23 with yet another very cerebral piece from *Sgt. Peppers.*' This one was never a single release, but it was one of the most popular songs from the album.

Buddha: As John Lennon picks off lyrical ideas from the *Daily Mail* newspaper of January 17, 1967, we hear of mundane road repairs, a fatal traffic accident and a movie review of a film in which he was actually in titled, *How I Won the War*. Paul contributes the middle bit about waking up and getting a typical day started.

DJ Eddie: But what does it all mean?

Buddha: In the big picture, what in life really matters? Is life a mere collection of daily events such as potholes and fatal car accidents? Is there a dimension beyond just the everyday hum-drum?

DJ Eddie: So what do you think John is telling us in this song, from your perspective?

Buddha: In an extremely artistic and creative way, John demonstrates: A wise man, recognizing that the world is but an illusion, does not act as if it were real, so he escapes the suffering.

ABOUT THE MUSIC

DJ Eddie: Back in the day, everyone thought this song was about a wild drug trip.

Buddha: Yeah, I was there at the time as well. Remember, I'm quite a bit older than you.

DJ Eddie: Yeah, but you know, wasn't this just a song about getting high on marijuana? Ya know, grass, a doobie, Mary Jane.

Buddha: Mary *who?*

DJ Eddie: Mary Jane. You know, *weed!*

Buddha: Oh, you mean as in smokin' a joint? Well, art is always filled with double, triple or quadruple meanings I suppose.

To me, I prefer to take the spiritual approach to this song masterpiece. I too, like John Lennon, *"would love to turn you on,"* but to the Eightfold Path and the Four Noble Truths I discussed earlier. I don't need to get high to appreciate this song. In fact, drugs only keep us from pure thinking. And, believe *especially* me, pursuing the Eightfold Path is hard enough without being on drugs while doing it!

DJ Eddie: You always seem to come back to the same old Eightfold Path routine. Why don't you loosen up a bit?

Buddha: And why should I? Hey Dude, you need to get off of my cloud, I'm on *your* side, remember? The elimination of suffering is the only theme in life that really matters, the rest is all distraction, better known as "attachments," discussed earlier. But back to the music.

DJ Eddie: Arguably the most remembered track of *Sgt. Peppers'*, this final cut on side two of the original vinyl record places an exclamation point on this iconic album. One hardly knows where to start in discussing this piece. To begin with, *A Day in the Life* represents one of the most famous and well executed of all Lennon & McCartney collaborations. This was again truly a synergy of their teamwork occurring at one of their pivotal, all-time high points.

Your take on it?

Buddha: While John is clearly the lead composer, both his verse lyrics and vocal treatment are utterly superb. The stage is set quietly and beautifully for Paul's contrasted fast-paced middle section or "break" in the song, wherein he wakes up to an alarm, falls out of bed and goes about his morning routine inside reality.

Within all this, the surreal, unforgettable magic happens in this artistic masterpiece: Paul had the idea to just leave two very long, silent "break" sections in the song. Even Paul himself wasn't quite sure what to do with these silent spaces at first. Later, he got the idea for a full orchestra to just play up the musical scale, but in a random fashion, without any sheet music. This, to classically trained orchestra members, was unheard of, of course. At EMI studios, Paul himself conducted the players to get the ultimate desired effect.

DJ Eddie: So how would you sum this all up?

Buddha: The unprecedented result, no doubt all have heard, is left to your ears and mind to describe. To me, this masterpiece represents all that is chaos in the world.

THE TRIVIA

DJ Eddie: After hearing Paul's idea to bring in the London Symphony Orchestra, for the up to now "silent break sections," producer Martin saw an already *way* over-budget album going further into the red. He knew from history he was certainly going to hear about it from the upper management at EMI.

But Martin had yet another most timely idea in hiring only half the symphony orchestra, then multi-track four different recorded takes to make the resulting sound much more full. With the able assistance of grossly underrated engineer, Geoff Emerick, it worked! By the way, for those interested, Emerick has written a really fascinating book on his in-studio engineering days with the Beatles entitled, *Here, There and Everywhere*. A must *read* for Beatles' aficionados.

Buddha: I've read it too and can recommend it. Emerick was a genius nested within a group of geniuses, all working toward the same goal. While George Martin was the well regarded "fifth Beatle," Emerick was the far less known "sixth Beatle," I might add.

DJ Eddie: Back in the recording studio the stage was set. Everyone was dressed to the hilt with men in black tie and tuxedo with tails, and women in psychedelic mini-skirt glory. The whole scene was one wild affair. So wild in fact, that Martin had to relinquish, gladly, I'm betting, the conducting of the orchestra to Paul.

Buddha: Sounds like a pretty wild time, all right. As I recollect, I'm pretty sure I was invited to this party, but I just couldn't make it that night (he winks).

DJ Eddie: For the recording session involving these now iconic break sections, Paul invited all the orchestral players present to wear Beatle-supplied disguises like rubber noses, bushy eyebrows, weirdo eyeglasses, bald head caps and so forth. After which, it was only then Paul explained that they were all to play their respective instruments, in random time, up the musical scale from their instrument's lowest note to its highest note. He got looks back of sheer bewilderment from these classically trained virtuosos. *Do what?*

Eventually, after numerous takes, the musicians got it.

Meanwhile, in studio and during the actual recording session, a party was raging the likes of which the very stuffy and conservative EMI executives had never seen, before or since. Adding to the festivities, many friends of the Beatles had been invited to this most unique, if unprofessional, session. Amidst the mayhem were guests including the Rolling Stones' Mick Jagger and Brian Jones. Also included were Beatles' wives, other roadies and various associates.

Buddha: I was invited too, but I was called out of town to a yoga convention in Sedona, Arizona. But, musically, in the end, Paul got the hugely orchestrated break sections he wanted and it *is* absolutely brilliant.

DJ Eddie: The entire song, a true Beatles' masterpiece, ends on a final chord (E major). This was added later and played on three pianos in the studio. Paul, George Martin and Ringo hit the same E chord simultaneously, while engineer, Emerick, recorded the resulting sound for the longest possible audible carry, over 40 seconds until complete fade out. If you listen very, very carefully, headphones will help, you can hear Ringo shift and scape his folding chair along the studio floor as the E-chord fades out and thus, ends the track.

So, is all this *finally* the end befitting the *Sgt. Peppers'* album? No, not quite! Paul had no less yet *another* idea, this time to put a high-pitched dog whistle sound and some backwards talking at the very end, known as the "out groove" of the vinyl. Whew!

Buddha: Well, if we ever needed an example of thinking "outside the box," this is certainly it. Look at the power unleashed when you go a different route away from the norms. The path of genius is never heavily traveled, nor is the path to full spirituality and peace of mind. But it is always worth it.

The most famous drum kit in history?

25: All You Need Is Love
(Lennon 90%, McCartney 5%, Harrison 5%)

DJ Eddie: This one is certainly one of John Lennon's most famous compositions. I'm sure you've got a lot to say about this tune, yes?

Buddha: Hatred does not cease by hatred, but only by love. This is the eternal rule.

A cornerstone tenet of my philosophy is the basis of this lyric by John. Virtually anything is possible, and there are no boundaries for those whose outlook is filled with love. Similar in theme to Paul's, *Here, There and Everywhere* cited earlier, love is all encompassing and it is everywhere, in everyone and in everything, including the entire cosmos around you. If you communicate with the world around you by just giving and receiving love, you truly will have it all. Importantly, this concept is an extremely simple one, but getting there, especially in today's world, can be a complex challenge.

Love is most powerful and is nested within both a personal and worldly universe, as beautifully represented here in John's song. The deepest of messages is presented in a very simple communicative and musical form. From the Eightfold Path, I speak specifically of Right Thought, or visualization, and Right Knowledge, or becoming one with the world. Love is the vehicle that gets you there.

But can it all actually be this simple and basic? If we open ourselves up wide enough to see it, then, yes in fact, love is all you need.

ABOUT THE MUSIC

DJ Eddie: Go cat, go! Man, you sure know how to explain this stuff! To me, this seems like just a cute, "pie in the sky," unrealistic lyric without any practical meaning. I mean, I just see Woodstock and dancing girls with flowers in their hair. And the music seems so simple.

Buddha: Well, there's nothing entirely wrong with dancing girls with flowers in their hair and yes, it is a very simple tune, musically speaking. And the simple melody fits well with the very simple, but universal message. It's the *carrying out* of the message in daily life that is so tough. The melody is very catchy and the song is nearly impossible not to sing along with. This was clearly John's intent.

DJ Eddie: This song also served as the perfect Beatles' music video for *Our World*, a live BBC broadcast and global hook-up, done on June 25, 1967.

Although now commonplace, this broadcast was yet another Beatles' "first" as live satellite connections for a pop music performance was virtually unheard of at the time.

In the music video, the boys, in actuality, are singing live to their prerecorded studio music tracks, recorded weeks earlier. John's singing appears very nonchalant throughout his lead vocal, but his performance is stellar.
In retrospect, John admitted to being a bit nervous during the broadcast, but you would have never known it. The other Beatles commented too that this was pure John in his element. In other words, when the pressure was on, John always came through.

Buddha: As the recording fades out, one can hear Paul chanting in the background, "*She loves you, yeah, yeah, yeah!*" in perfect time in between John's lead vocal lines. This is a very clever reference of course to the 1964 Beatles' hit single and Paul fits it in only as a musical genius could!

THE TRIVIA

DJ Eddie: Transmitted from the EMI studio on Abbey Road, the Beatles again took an opportunity to invite their friends to their performance. Among the floating balloons on the set, there were many notables in the party crowd, a few of whom can be seen in the video, including Mick Jagger, Keith Moon, Marianne Faithful and Eric Clapton.

Buddha: Yeah, I was invited to this one too, but that night I was the keynote speaker at the annual Truth in Advertising Convention in Las Vegas.

In the video, we also see some different instruments, part of the *Magical Mystery Tour* era: Paul, sitting to John's right, is playing a Rickenbacker 4001 bass instead of his "mop top" era, Hofner violin bass. To John's left, George, sporting bright orange pants with shoes to match, is playing his formerly sonic blue, now psychedelic Fender Stratocaster named "Rocky." Ringo fashions quite a new look and the famous "dropped-T" BeaTles logo is no longer found on his Ludwig bass drum, marking the new Beatles' era. As for John, he is center stage wearing his headphones and listening to the musical tracks he is singing along to, chewing gum all the while!

DJ Eddie: Chewing gum?

Buddha: Hey, John Lennon could do whatever he wanted!

Recording in the controlled environment of a private studio is one thing, but performing live in an around-the-world broadcast from the BBC was yet another. Producer Martin and trusty first engineer, Emerick, were under intense pressure for this first-ever, live music transmission. A slip-up in anyway would surely have caused horrific, governmental embarrassment for the Beatles, their EMI/Parlaphone record label, the entire EMI management and technical staff.

Years later in a documentary, Martin admitted that he was sweating bullets, praying for no errors, especially when a routinely unpredictable John Lennon was involved as the lead singer. Aside from those worries, just before show time, Emerick too was exasperated with temperamental audio equipment and malfunctioning tape playback pin connections. While backstage, Martin and Emerick were nerve-wracked but once on-camera the Fab Four performed the song flawlessly. To this day, this five-minute extravaganza is a great example of an early and fun music video.

DJ Eddie: Friends, it's time for another short commercial break brought to you by Buddha. We'll be right back to continue our Beatles' marathon.

Commercial Break

Buddha: Hi folks. Time for a relaxing vacation? Not to be confused with that other resort, now instead try my not new and completely unimproved resort: Robe and Sandals. No suitcase, passport, taxi, shuttle bus, aircraft, rental car or hotel required. You don't spend a dime. Close your eyes, breathe deeply and let yourself go totally calm. Welcome to *meditation*. It will take some practice, but soon you'll be really racking up a million frequent tranquility miles without flying anywhere.

Too weird? Too good to be true? Yeah, I understand, but just try it. Start slowly and be amazed at where you "go."

26: The Inner Light

(Harrison 95%, McCartney 5%)

DJ Eddie: We're back from your commercial message that segues into our next tune on your hit parade, *The Inner Light*. I see you've picked another very little known Beatles' track for your number 26. I've met very few people in my DJ work that have ever even heard of this song.

Buddha: I know it might seem a strange pick, but George nails this one, right smack on target, especially in light of the commercial break I just presented. In fact, in this song, lyrically, I couldn't have conveyed the message better. As George travels deeper into Eastern spirituality, his lyrics grow even more intense and all powerful. This song is about nothing less than the culmination of the Eightfold Path at its highest level, Right Knowledge.

His, and my, basic message is simply this: most people are just trying too hard at all the wrong things and they easily lose their way. Through self-understanding, via meditation, you can and *will* discover all there is to know in this life.

DJ Eddie: Whoa, these are ultra-heavy lyrics for a Western culture pop song, but then again, with George, we're not dealing with just some ordinary songwriter.

But how do I know when I arrive at the place George is talking about?

Buddha: You are not *there*, at Nirvana. That's why you are here, on earth. You will work things out on earth and return numerous times to the cosmos until you do get it figured out. Once you have eliminated suffering, which is entirely caused by your attachments, you will no longer need to be here and you will be there.

DJ Eddie: Oh Daddy-O! It sounds like we're back to your Eightfold Path again.

Buddha: Right Knowledge is the bottom line of the Eightfold Path. Have *that* and you've got *The Inner Light*, indeed. Go George!"

ABOUT THE MUSIC

DJ Eddie: Deeply rooted in Eastern music, the song demonstrates a real combination of diverse musical forms combined with a unique melody. George's lead vocal treatment is excellent as well as he gets the message across with a delicate vibe befitting the backdrop of the music.

Buddha: If you have not listened carefully to these lyrics, you are missing something very special. While sitar is the lead instrument throughout, the song is presented in a series of starts and stops that is most intriguing. It's hard to put your finger on all that is going on during this track, but somehow it all works out beautifully.

THE TRIVIA

Buddha: George and John appeared on the television show *The Frost Report* (hosted by David Frost) on September 29, 1967. The discussion focused on the power of meditation. In the audience was one Juan Mascaro, a Cambridge professor, who after the show sent George a book of Eastern thought that he had edited titled, *Lamps of Fire*. Mascaro also suggested that George consider the poem, *"The Inner Light"* from the Tao Te Ching. Enough said. George was on it like spiritual glue!

DJ Eddie: *The Inner Light* was the very first time a Harrison song was ever on a Beatles' 45rpm vinyl, as it appeared as the B-side to *Lady Madonna* in March of 1968. Paul has made a point of saying how much he loved this particular effort from George. To this day, *The Inner Light* is one of the most obscure and under-rated of all Beatles' officially released recordings.

27: The Fool on the Hill
(McCartney, 100%)

Buddha: Whether Paul knows it or not, and I believe he does, in this song he has painted a picture of Zen meditation. While explaining that the man on the hill is a fool as perceived by others, the truth is that he is seeking wisdom through quiet time and meditation. While seeing the "world go 'round," the man watches the sunset and is obviously in deep contemplation. Yes, the "fool" is moving on the path of Enlightenment. It can be a lonely path that few others in the world understand. So it is too with my Buddhist philosophy.

Do what you have to do resolutely, with all your heart. The traveler who hesitates only raises dust on the road.

DJ Eddie: Yo' mama! I see this now. You are right on, man!

Buddha: Yeah, yeah, yeah, I know. But instead of "right on, man," think Right Concentration and Right Thought, as implied strongly by this song. As previously discussed, both ultimately lead to Right Knowledge and Nirvana. You literally just can't do any better than that. Nice work in composing this, Sir Paul.

ABOUT THE MUSIC

DJ Eddie: Paul wrote the song on his own while with John at the latter's home on Cavendish Avenue. It is a very simple song chord-wise with an added solo flute as the instrument of main focus throughout. The song's music video, shot overlooking Nice, France, is one of the highlights in the Beatles' "home movie" of late 1967, *Magical Mystery Tour*.

THE TRIVIA

Buddha: Long-time Beatles' associate and renowned author, Alistair Taylor, recalls an event just hours before Paul's penning of this song. Alistair and Paul were walking Paul's dog, Martha, one in the same which inspired Paul's song, *Martha My Dear*, on the Beatles' *White Album*. Both Alistair and Paul had momentarily lost the pooch amongst rolling hills in the countryside and they were getting very concerned. From out of nowhere, a man appeared and happily returned Martha to them. Greetings were exchanged between the three gentlemen and just as suddenly as the man appeared, he literally disappeared.

A stunned Paul turned to Alistair, "Did this just happen? Did that man really just vanish into thin air?" Alistair concurred that the meeting did in fact occur. They concluded that this must have been some sort of spiritual experience, defying any other reasonable definition. It is widely assumed that it was this mysterious event that immediately acted as the catalyst for Paul's composition. In answer to Paul's question, from my high-level inside information, yeah, this was a spiritual experience!

The Magical Mystery Tour bus

28: Hey Jude
(90% McCartney, 5% Lennon, 5% Harrison)

Buddha: In this poignant, almost gospel-like song, Paul describes how life is really all about your perspective on things. The bottom line is that comfort, reassurance, compassion, understanding, acceptance and ultimately, love are the keys to a successful life. No matter who or what comes your way, the path of love is all healing, but you've got to put in the Right Effort to make it happen.

How? Let go of anger. Let go of pride. When you are bound by nothing you go beyond sorrow.

I often speak of Right Effort, and the *Hey Jude* lyrical messages fit into my philosophy exactly. Put in all the Right Effort toward other people and things and the world will open up to you.

DJ Eddie: Hey Dude, you are one cool cat. Tell us about *Hey Jude*.

ABOUT THE MUSIC

Buddha: The song, of course, is an all-time Beatles' classic within their classics. Using an almost amazingly simple chord structure, the song was the most popular Beatles' tune of all-time selling over five million 45rpm vinyl records worldwide in just a few *weeks*.

Since that time, if anything, the tune has become even more popular. Still performed live today by Sir Paul on tour, the song immediately evokes a full audience sing-a-long, whether in the U.K., the USA, or even at Red Square in Moscow. Universal appeal, indeed.

THE TRIVIA

DJ Eddie: Originally titled, *Hey Julian*, Paul's lyrics are aimed directly at John's son of the same name. While John and Cynthia were in divorce proceedings and with Yoko Ono's strong ever-presence in the studio and everywhere else, Julian was caught helplessly in all the family discord.

Buddha: I might add that during this time and even before, Paul had grown very close to Julian, so close in fact that Julian had later discussed how he felt closer to "uncle" Paul than to his own father. It was actually sometime later that Paul had revealed to John that the song lyrics were meant as unsolicited advice to Julian. You guessed it: Right Speech, Right Thought and Right Actions, yet again.

29: While My Guitar Gently Weeps
(Harrison 100%)

Buddha: George hits yet another home run with this one! In a deeply philosophical way, the "quiet Beatle" talks about the faults and sadness within mankind and the ever-present suffering.

DJ Eddie: Holy lava lamp, here you go again with the "suffering" bit…

Buddha: Eddie, Eddie, *Eddie!* It's not a "bit." Suffering is everywhere and I'm out to *eliminate* it. You make it sound like I'm *for* suffering. I spent most of life figuring out ways to eliminate it, so give me a break.

You say you think you're getting it, so listen up: It is imperative that people stay open to the world around them and at the same time learn from their mistakes. There is sadness and crying involved as learning can be very painful. From an outside observer's standpoint, George reflects on why we have created such a world of sorrow and how the suffering continues, seemingly endlessly.

As said earlier, suffering is the basis of my Four Noble Truths, the foundation of Buddhist philosophy. George's lyrics fit exactly and I couldn't agree more with his observations and sentiment. Moreover, the whole point to my philosophy is to *end all of the suffering* that George is writing about.

You cannot travel the path until you have become the path itself. Have compassion for all beings, the rich and poor alike as each has their suffering. Some suffer too much, others too little, but all on earth suffer by way of their attachments. That's why you are all still here, on earth.

ABOUT THE MUSIC

Buddha: A gorgeous musical masterpiece, this one. While the Beatles were having their intense inner personal struggles during the *White Album* sessions throughout 1968, George was busy stockpiling compositions, of which this was one. During this period, John and Paul were working largely independently as well and George's songs were being generally "set aside" by the group, to put it kindly.

DJ Eddie: I can add here that as to the famous *White Album* released version of this song, John and Paul were showing little interest in working on it, so George countered with an unprecedented move: on a casual whim, one July morning, he asked his good friend, Eric Clapton, to come down to the studio with him and track in some lead guitar over the existing piano, guitar, organ with Leslie speaker, drum, tambourine and bass tracks.

Buddha: Understandably, Eric was extremely apprehensive: *"Me?* Play on a *Beatles'* record? You must be joking. No one's ever done that!" George replied, "Well, it's my song and I would like you to play on it." So, it came to be. The resulting Clapton lead guitar track is astonishing and it serves this brilliant piece well.

Our lesson? Think outside the box. In uncomfortable situations or in considering things that just haven't been tried before, always stay open to new ideas. George and Eric did!

THE TRIVIA

Buddha: This puppy is right down my alley, or Ashram, as it were.

George was inspired by the *I Ching,* also known as the ancient Chinese *"Book of Changes,"* and began to apply it to his songwriting, with this composition being a particularly good case in point.

While My Guitar Gently Weeps started out life as a very slow and moody acoustic guitar piece, with producer, Martin, adding light orchestration, most notably some melancholy cello lines. In fact, that version appeared years later on the Beatles' *Anthology* compact disc series and it's quite good, too! George knew he had a winner with this song and continued to work it. Eventually the song evolved into the final released version we know and love.

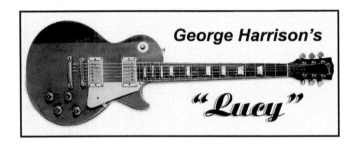

George's Gibson Les Paul guitar, played by Eric Clapton on *While My Guitar Gently Weeps*

30: **Dear Prudence**
(Lennon, 90%, McCartney 10%)

DJ Eddie: We're all the way up to number 30 now on Buddha's hit parade.

Buddha: Hiding from the world is not an answer. Instead, it is imperative to come out and experience all the beauty in the universe around you. This is the basic message of *Dear Prudence*.

I again speak of Right Effort and Right Actions are a part of the Eightfold Path. It is crucial for individuals to put their efforts and actions into the cosmos and contribute to it. I also speak of meditation in terms of Right Mindfulness and Right Concentration, but only to the extent that it is healthful and helpful. These are the many principles alluded to in this great composition by John.

ABOUT THE MUSIC

Buddha: Written by John Lennon in Rishikesh, India, while studying under Maharishi Mahesh Yogi, the song starts with a simple, but captivating, acoustic guitar riff and melodic vocal line. As the song progresses, it's music tracks build significantly, culminating in a final verse and chorus of outstanding musical accompaniment, highlighted particularly with Paul's, yes, Paul's, not Ringo's, intricate drum work.

THE TRIVIA

Buddha: Actress Mia Farrow's younger sister, Prudence, was reclusive while attending the meditations at Rishikesh. She had reportedly locked herself in a room for three weeks for the purposes of deep meditation.

Fellow attendees, the Maharishi and one John Lennon were all getting quite concerned about her welfare. Eventually, Prudence did come out and participate in talk sessions with John, George and Donovan.

Greatly flattered, Prudence said later that she had never heard the song until after it came out on the *White Album*. Most appropriately, Prudence is today residing in the Florida sun and, I'm most happy to report, is a teacher of meditation.

DJ Eddie: Back to our show in just a minute after a quick commercial break from Buddha.

Commercial Break

Buddha: You scrub those kitchen pots and pans until they are shiny new. Now, *you* too can become spotless, shining from within and forever and never mind the current mileage on your mind or body.

Just like cleaning your pots and pans, it will take a bit of elbow grease on your part, call it Right Effort, but you *can* get to shiny, new Nirvana. You will amaze your friends as you work yourself into that reincarnated *you!*

George and Ringo with Maharishi Mahesh Yogi

31: The Continuing Story of Bungalow Bill
(Lennon, 100%)

DJ Eddie: We're back to the show. But Buddha, buzz off, will ya? What does the shooting and killing of an innocent animal got to do with you, of all people?

Buddha: In this biting sarcasm, John brilliantly, yet gently through humor, exposes the folly of mankind in the hunting and killing of other living things for sport. If not directly for purposes of Right Livelihood, senseless killing is neither Right Effort nor Right Action. Such behaviors can never lead to Right Knowledge and Nirvana.

ABOUT THE MUSIC

DJ Eddie: The song is a cousin of John's earlier *Yellow Submarine* composition as it is one part children's humor combined with one part simple sing-along. Think also: *All You Need Is Love* and *Give Peace a Chance*, both Lennon hallmarks as well.

The introductory classical guitar riff is supplied by John's mellotron (an early electronic keyboard synthesizer of sorts). This mellotron was also used in the intro of *Strawberry Fields Forever*, in the latter as played by Paul. But Buddha, what else do you know about the tune?

THE TRIVIA

Buddha: I had some inside information on this one, since it all happened near my home town in India. While there, partaking in the Maharishi's meditation course, John had the opportunity to meet one Richard Cooke III and his mother, Nancy. From Texas, John saw Cooke as the quintessential American college boy.

DJ Eddie: So how did they get from there to shooting a tiger?

Buddha: After an afternoon's hunting trip in which Cooke, with his mother assisting, shot and killed a tiger, they both attended a talk session with John, George and the Maharishi. As John learned of the hunt, he was incensed. John compared the hunt to the adventures of America's folk hero, Buffalo Bill, then wrote and titled the song accordingly.

As to John's anger, I can only say that holding on to anger is like grasping a hot coal with the intent of throwing it at someone else, like Cooke in this case. You are the only one who gets burned.

Said another way: you will not be punished *for* your anger, but you will be punished *by* your anger.

As for Mr. Cooke, he had terrible regret over killing the tiger, while mum Nancy still contended it "would have been us instead of him," as per John's song lyric. Years later, once his identity was known, Cooke continued to receive postcards from all over the world asking what he had killed lately. Today, he works as a photographer for *National Geographic*.

And speaking of shooting things, don't shoot the messenger, the Maharishi. His message of meditation was paramount, even if he fell victim to the frailties of being human on occasion. Nobody's perfect, unless their residence address is Nirvana Avenue.

Although synthesizers are not generally associated with Beatles' music, here's a very early model of a Moog as used in 1967-70, mainly by an avant-garde George Harrison. Hear this Moog predominantly used in the songs Here Comes the Sun, Because, It's All Too Much and It's Only a Northern Song.

32: Revolution
(Lennon 85%, McCartney 15%)

Buddha: Continuous change is part of life, but violence is just not the way to do it. You can not eliminate violence by creating it. Sadly, few in the world seem to understand this tenet. Conversely, the path to peaceful change is filled with Buddhist principles of Right Speech, Right Thought, Right Effort and Right Action, and they all come into play here.

If you fight fire with fire, you end up only with ashes.

DJ Eddie: You are really freaking me out, Buddha. "Fighting fire with fire and ending up only with ashes," is such a spiritual way to look at it. I love it.

Buddha: Yes and the cosmos loves you, too.

ABOUT THE MUSIC

DJ Eddie: Having gone through a major revision, *Revolution* was more of a musical *evolution*! Started as a slow tempo, acoustic guitar number, the boys weren't sure the song was what they wanted. Yoko Ono, by now, a bona fide recording session resident, complete with her in-studio bed, chimed in by commenting that this first recorded version of *Revolution* was far too slow. Wait a second. Who asked *her*?

Buddha: To the Beatles credit, Yoko was not thrown out on her ear. Instead, by using Right Thought and Right Concentration, the boys re-recorded a new up-tempo, highly electric version which became the popular 45rpm single. Meanwhile, the slow version appears on the *White Album* as the re- titled, *Revolution One*.

DJ Eddie: I might add here that the song *Revolution Number Nine*, also on the White Album, is an altogether different track, showcasing John and Yoko as they travel into avant-garde territory.

Buddha: That's John. He was always thinking outside the box. Yes, this can be controversial, when and if, the public doesn't understand your direction or intent. What I call Right Understanding, seeing things as they really are, and without fear, is the key here.

THE TRIVIA

Buddha: Speaking of the avant-garde Revolution Number Nine, John was adamant about this being the A-side of the next Beatles' single release. Producer Martin and Paul, together with George and Ringo, presumably, were shocked and greatly distressed at this suggestion.

DJ Eddie: Yeah, I guess Yoko's studio bed-in was bad enough, but now had John completely lost it? *Revolution Number Nine* was pretty far out even for Beatles' aficionados, and you certainly couldn't sing along to it!

As far as the next single release, John was almost immediately overruled as *Hey Jude* became the 45rpm vinyl, with the fast-paced *Revolution* appearing as the B-side.

Buddha: If you're looking for something new, whether it's in a guitar sound or in a life philosophy, it's going to take a certain amount of experimentation.

Example? For the "fast-paced" Revolution, John had asked engineer, Emerick, for the most over-the-top distortion possible from John's Epiphone Casino hollow body rhythm guitar. Emerick, the engineer genius he was, nicely accommodated John by plugging the guitar directly through the mixing board preamps to beyond the point of outlandish overload. Emerick was convinced he would have been fired for this crazed technique had the EMI studio bosses known about it.

So yes, John got his supersonic guitar sound. Just listen to the lead-in notes of this track! Caution: Don't blow your speakers or eardrums!

As to Buddhist philosophy, this too may be a new experiment for you. But the results may be just as supersonic!

33: The Long and Winding Road
(McCartney 100% or McCartney 65%, Spector 30%, Lennon 5%, depending on how you want to look at it.)

DJ Eddie: Hey cats, we're up to Buddha's number 33, closing toward the end of our show. This one is a really pretty production, yes? Buddha, what's your take on it?

Buddha: Groovy, far out and, man-alive, I'm practically speechless over this song.

On a long journey of human life, *faith* is the best companion because it is the best refreshment on the journey.

Life is a long journey, a "long and winding road" indeed. It's the "winding" part that makes it all so fascinating. The truth is, we never really know what is around that next curve, although sometimes we think we have it all figured out. It is usually exactly then that life surprises us, sometimes with wonderful detours and sometimes with very challenging ones.

I continuously speak of Right Livelihood, Right Effort and Right Action throughout life's winding road, but what is *your* destination and how do you want to travel? What philosophy will lead you to *your* door?" You don't necessarily need my philosophy to get there, but everybody's gonna need some kind of spiritual base to operate from or that long and winding road leads nowhere!

ABOUT THE MUSIC

Buddha: If Paul has ever written a sweeter melody, the world would love to hear it. The original piece was recorded by Paul as a simple demo for the *Let It Be* film, with Paul doing a solo lead vocal while at the piano and John, quite uncharacteristically, playing bass.

DJ Eddie: It's pretty obvious in watching the movie that the band is a disintegrating mess by this point. So sad.

Buddha: Not so sad. Everything has a start and an end, only to start again, in another form in the cosmos. In reality, there is no beginning and no end. The Beatles were not going to last forever either, so in this movie we were witness to the beginning of their demise. But don't equate demise with sadness, it's just part of life. "*Let It Be,*" indeed!

Later, with the movie released to lukewarm reviews and the band in total disarray, this song in a demo version surfaced only on numerous, poor quality,

Beatles' bootleg albums of the day. An official Beatles' album from the movie was still unforeseen as the band basically, but unofficially, ceased to exist, at least for the time being.

DJ Eddie: Through a long series of legal and personal events, too numerous and complex to go into here, the Beatles were in serious turmoil. During this time, Paul and John were practically estranged from each other. Contractually required to create an album release, on behalf of the Beatles, John hired world famous producer, Phil Spector, to salvage some of the *Let It Be* session tapes.

Unbeknownst to Paul, *The Long and Winding Road* on the *Let It Be* album and as a 45rpm single, were both released in May 1970, only after Spector's layering in of strings, horns and choir over Paul's original demo recording. Paul was said to be absolutely furious over an outside producer, even one of Spector's renowned stature, touching his material without his consent.

Buddha: Eddie, I must add here that Phil Spector's iconic "wall of sound" production of this song, given the almost primitive nature of the original demo he had to work with, is quite remarkable, if not astonishing. It must also be noted that had John not brought in Spector, most of the world to this day may never had heard this astonishingly beautiful song. Make no mistake, Right Concentration and Right Effort, in the form of amazing focus and hard work by Phil, made it happen.

The Long and Winding Road was a huge hit record. The song is heralded to this day as just another one of Paul's seemingly endless, outstanding ballads.

THE TRIVIA

DJ Eddie: Paul wrote the song inspired by his farm and surroundings near Campeltown and Kintyre, Scotland. The imagery of rain, wind and a winding road are all part of Paul's remote farm environment. In fact, it is speculated that the actual "winding road" is Highway B842, comprised of 16 miles of turns running down the east coast of Kintyre.

34: Let It Be
(McCartney 80%, Lennon 10%, Harrison 10%)

DJ Eddie: You just spoke of the *Let it Be* album and now here's the single by the same name at number 34 on your list.

Buddha: In yet another colossal, almost gospel-like piece, Paul salutes his own mother, Mary, and her "words of wisdom." In the most deeply personal way, Paul acknowledges that everyone needs support and guidance, especially in dark hours of despair or fear.

There is great power in positive thought, words and speech. We're talking no less than Right Speech, Right Thought, Right Effort and Right Understanding.

DJ Eddie: Four critical elements of your Eightfold Path in one song? You are blowing my mind!

Buddha: Oh, calm down.

As a corollary, the *Let It Be* lyrics can also be taken as excellent advice in dealing with the world around us every day. The fundamental idea here is one of acceptance of the earthly things that you cannot change. Better to find strength inside yourself than to just become more frustrated with the things you cannot do anything about. If you can truly "let it be" you have taken a big step toward ultimate wisdom.

In Buddhist philosophy, I talk a great deal about all the elements of the Eightfold Path, and *Let It Be* reflects many of these. I can only add, with deepest respect, that Paul's mother, Mary, was a *very* wise mother indeed.

ABOUT THE MUSIC

DJ Eddie: Almost a gospel tune, Paul's beautiful, yet simple melody is led by piano. There are two versions of the song. On the 45rpm single, a break fill is supplied by an organ played through the usual EMI studio-based Leslie speaker, while a second version of the song features an excellent, biting guitar Harrison lead in the same break. It should be noted that these two versions of *Let It Be* might be the same recording, but mixed quite differently.

Buddha: I hear ya. Beauty comes in many different versions, but you've gottta recognize it, which means you gotta be looking for it!

THE TRIVIA

Buddha: The "despair" Paul is referring to in this song was the seemingly inevitable break-up of the Beatles. But we all know that despair is inevitable at many points in life.

The "Mary" referred to in the song is Paul's deceased mother, although most listeners assume he is speaking of the Virgin Mary, which is totally untrue. Let It Be was the Beatles' last 45rpm single, released in March of 1970.

Fender Esquire guitar heard on the intro and reprise of the song, Sgt. Peppers Lonely Hearts Club Band, as played by Paul. An extremely early, rare and valuable guitar from 1951, Paul had to modify it for his left-handed playing.

35: I, Me, Mine

(Harrison 100%)

DJ Eddie: For number 35, I see you are back to a George Harrison tune.

Buddha: And why not? The song is brilliant.

George is professing another sharp attack on materialism and, moreover, egocentric behavior. Coming from "rock star icon" status, it certainly is not easy to balance material wealth with the bigger spiritual picture. As would anyone in such circumstances, George struggled with this, or perhaps better said, he was very wise to even recognize the inherent spiritual conflicts integral to being a world figure. To his credit, the pinnacle of the Eightfold Path, Right Knowledge, was obviously approaching him fast. George was an older soul with very little left to learn in this life.

Were there a mountain all made of gold, doubled, that would not be enough to satisfy a single man. Know this and live accordingly.

DJ Eddie: Yeah, but I want a raise and that new Mercedes. You know, that latest model with the windshield wipers and washers for the headlights! Am I doomed?

Buddha: Many people have begun to see the light, but unfortunately, are not quite there yet. Once you can step outside of yourself, see your worldly wants and needs as less than essential, then you are approaching the final reward.

Said another way, when the person is ready, the Right Knowledge will appear. At that point, you are *ultimately* wealthy and will, in fact, own it all.

ABOUT THE MUSIC

DJ Eddie: Together with numerous starts and stops, this quite musically intricate rocker holds up with the best of them. George lets loose with some excellent electric guitar work encapsulated in a driving rhythm section. Ringo's drum work here is flawless and moves the song in a perfect tempo through numerous starts and stops.

Buddha: I sense that George's lead vocal is truly heartfelt. You can feel it in his delivery of the lines: this man really *means* what he is saying! If it walks like a Buddhist and talks like a Buddhist…

THE TRIVIA

Buddha: *I, Me, Mine* is not just George preaching about the woes of self-centered behavior to others. He saw *himself* as part of the conflicted masses as well. In quite a humbling way, he is giving loving advice to himself as well as to others: Escape from the conceit, "I am." This is the highest happiness.

DJ Eddie: Yeah, I think I get it. Maybe my new Mercedes can wait.

Buddha: It's just an attachment. I'm not impressed.

DJ Eddie: Back to the music. Odd as it seems, let me add that as to the interesting and unconventional waltz time of the song, George was inspired by an Austrian marching band broadcast he heard over a BBC radio program.

Hey fans, we'll be back in a minute after a short commercial message. You've hung in this long, so stick with us for another few minutes as we conclude our interview with Buddha here at KOMM.

Commercial Break

Buddha: Iron poor blood? You don't need a transfusion. You need not any supplements or chemistry lab-developed pills by Big Pharm, either.

As a famous band once said: all you need is love.

So try my not-so-secret spiritual formula, with recipes available at better bookstores everywhere. And tell 'em Buddha sent ya.

George's Fender Stratocaster, repainted by the artist himself and named "Rocky." This guitar was featured particularly during the Magical Mystery Tour era but was also used (in Fender's original "sonic blue" factory color) by both John and George in earlier eras.

36: **Get Back**
(McCartney 80%, Lennon 10%, Harrison 10%)

DJ Eddie: Back to the show! Buddha, how about this one? An interesting title to the song, but what exactly are we getting back *to*?

Buddha: As this song directs, we all need to get back to our true roots, "*where you belong*." Although Paul's lyric here is playful and humorous, he has essentially, intended or not, hit on a much deeper meaning.

Through Right Concentration and Right Mindfulness via meditation, we need to first find, then own up to, our true roots and beliefs. Through this understanding, we create a solid base from which we can most effectively live our daily lives. When faced with challenging dilemmas in our lives, we must be able to get back to our roots and deepest principles.

In my philosophy, you just keep getting back to the cosmos until you work it all out and reach Right Knowledge at the end of the Eightfold Path. In fact, you most precisely get back to exactly where you belong.

DJ Eddie: Holy eternity, man, you don't miss a beat, Daddy-O!

ABOUT THE MUSIC

DJ Eddie: *Get Back* was played live on the rooftop of the Apple's building in London. Beatles' fans remember well this final Beatles' concert as the closing sequence to the movie, *Let It Be*. A relatively simple tune with Paul singing lead, the song with its bouncy and catchy melody, has been a longtime fan favorite. Also of note, John adds some tasty guitar riffs while George plays excellent rhythm guitar and Ringo has an interesting short drum break. Paul plays his usual, great bass lines.

THE TRIVIA

DJ Eddie: There are two interesting trivia notes regarding the instrumentation in the live rooftop performance. First, we note Ringo's official final drum kit of the Beatles. Second, we see George (very uncharacteristically) playing a most interesting, rosewood Fender Telecaster. This one-of-a-kind "rosewood-Tele" has become a bit of a holy grail amongst guitar collectors and is still discussed to this day.

Buddha: Well, the instrumentation is interesting, but the song and band would be great almost regardless of the tools they used. It's not about the tangible, material stuff like guitars or drums. It's about the cerebral part of what's going on. It's about the best instrument of all, our creative minds.

37: Because
(Lennon 80%, McCartney 10%, Harrison 10%)

Buddha: Here, John holds gratitude for all the love and beauty nested in the world, including the simple non-material things like the sky and wind. I am most delighted to report that nothing could better represent my overall philosophy. Looking for inner peace? Love of all that surrounds you is *the* key. Wow, John scores *really* big here!

But neither fire nor wind, birth nor death can erase our good deeds.

DJ Eddie: So few people even know of this beautiful song.

Buddha: Yes, an unawareness of beauty is nested everywhere on this earth.

ABOUT THE MUSIC

DJ Eddie: I always liked the harmony sung on this one and it's really amazing how many people are unaware of this beautiful song from the *White Album*.

Buddha: Eddie, I agree with you. Using multiple and careful layering of vocal tracks, the harmony here is peerless. It is lush and beautiful in keeping with the song's message. *Because* seems musically flawless no matter how many times you listen to it.

THE TRIVIA

Buddha: While relaxing at home, John heard Yoko playing Beethoven's Piano *Sonata Number 14 in C-Sharp Minor*, better known as the famous *Moonlight Sonata*. John asked her to play the chords in a backward order and hence the chord structure of *Because* was born. By the way, John saw Beethoven as the "supreme composer."

DJ Eddie: Hmmm…, dude, I think this gives the pop classic *Roll Over, Beethoven* a whole new meaning!

38: Across the Universe
(Lennon 100%)

DJ Eddie: We're really closing fast now as we approach the end of your list and our interview. Here's number 38 on your hit parade.

Buddha: In this style of James Joyce, "stream of consciousness" lyric, John wonderfully expresses so many emotions and assembles it all into a beautiful ballad. The bottom line is that John recognizes and accepts all these emotions and sees that they are an inseparable part of his life. He is also adamant and even stubborn in that he won't allow anything to "change his world" within his own mind.

I must yet again allude to Right Thought, Right Concentration and Right Mindfulness as John indirectly addresses these principles in his poignant lyrics. As I said before, getting in touch with your feelings, accepting them and practicing meditation will lead to inner peace. As we discussed earlier, it's so simple, yet so hard. But it *can* be accomplished.

ABOUT THE MUSIC

DJ Eddie: There are two distinct versions of this very melodic and moody song. The first, recorded in February of 1968, begins with a flock of pigeons flying off and is laced with children singing in the chorus sections, "*nothing's gonna change my world.*" It was this recorded version that was generously donated as a fundraiser for the World Wildlife Fund in December 1969.

Buddha: Eddie, let me add that the second version of the song, the far more recognized, appears on the *Let It Be* album. John himself said that this was one of his own personal favorite songs because of the "purity of the lyrics." Hard to argue! The song is superb in both lyrical and melodic content.

THE TRIVIA

Buddha: While living in their Kenwood home, John was in a tumultuous period with his wife, Cynthia. Having difficulty sleeping, the phrase, "*pools of sorrow, waves of joy*" kept repeating through his head, so he thought he had better write it down before it slipped away. From this meager one phrase start, the rest of the song evolved.

DJ Eddie: John wanted this song to be the next Beatles' 45rpm single, but his wishes lost out to *Lady Madonna*.

39: Here Comes the Sun
(Harrison 100%)

DJ Eddie: Listeners, I'm afraid the sun is soon setting on our radio interview, but, at number 39, Buddha says the opposite!

Buddha: Reducing suffering is what my philosophy is all about. Replacing clouds and cold with bright sun provides an excellent metaphor in this regard with George's *Here Comes the Sun*.

DJ Eddie: The rising sun is actually a very cool thing, isn't it?

Buddha: In your culture "cool" and "hot" are kinda the same thing, so it all sort of bewilders me in a linguistic sense.

But the fundamental idea of optimism is really what this song is all about. Without such optimism, your future on earth is admittedly very grim. Only through positive thought and relaxation can the sun's warmth penetrate each of us, making us all *very* cool, to your way of talking! When I frequently speak of visualization in terms of Right Thought and Right Mindfulness leading to ultimately Right Knowledge, it is not a stretch to simply envision Geroge's rising sun melting the ice away.

ABOUT THE MUSIC

DJ Eddie: One of George's most recognized and beloved pieces, the song is built around an open D-chord played on an acoustic guitar. This introductory guitar riff is readily identifiable the world over today.

The center section of the song (the "middle eight") makes an interesting break with the rest of the song. Uplifting vocal harmonies bring out the positive vibe within the lyrics in this beautifully crafted production.

Buddha: As George sings, *"it's all right, it's all right, it's all right..."* Yes, it really is.

THE TRIVIA

Buddha: From Paul to Yoko to Lennons to lemonades, being immersed in troubling legal matters and chaos, George felt tremendous relief by escaping to a friend's house. That friend was Eric Clapton. While walking in Eric's garden, the sun came up and suddenly an overwhelming sense of optimism came over George, and *viola*, another Beatles' gem and international hit was born! There is beauty everywhere, everyday on earth. It surrounds us. Just look and see.

DJ Eddie: We've got just one tune left to round out Buddha's 40 Beatles' songs. Stay tuned, we'll be right back after this last break.

COMMERCIAL BREAK

Buddha: So gang, let's wrap it all up. There are eight basic parameters to understand, that Eightfold Path thing, basically. Live your life under those basic Buddhist teachings and you'll graduate! (See the Back Story.)

It might be time to mention that, at the risk of oversimplification, the Beatles answer to all this was encapsulated into one over-riding word: *love.*

The good news: As you get better at any one of the eight principles, the others tend to become easier to follow as well.

The bad news: Can you *really* live your life under these eight high-minded principles, given the video game-like mayhem when driving the freeways, waiting in a six-deep line at the supermarket, or hearing your neighbor's incessantly barking dog at 3AM? Hey, no one mentioned the word "easy" in this discussion. It's going to take work and commitment on your part.

Will striving to measure up to my Eightfold Path be worth it? That's a question you will need to look inside yourself to answer. But Buddhist thought says *what you don't learn in this life, you'll be back again another time to learn.* You'll keep coming back until you have nothing left to learn. At *that* point, you'll hit the eternal bliss of Nirvana with my mega- congratulations!

Some say that coming back again and again to the cosmos until you get it right sounds silly. Think about it. It seems to me that it is *more* silly to think that *this* life is more than just a one time shot. What would be the point of a one-time shot at life? We are much more significant than that. We came from the all powerful cosmos and we're staying in it to serve our purpose, whether you happen to like it or not.

Now, back to the show!

40: Medley: Golden Slumbers Carry That Weight The End

(McCartney 50%, Lennon 20%, Harrison 20%, Starr 10%)

DJ Eddie: Yo! That was some commercial break. Buddha, we're at the end of our show and this has been quite an adventure. I don't know what to say.

Buddha: Go with the feeling:

If you can't improve on the silence, say nothing. Let the greatest rock band in history say it for you. In fitting conclusion, the Beatles put together one last synergistic display of musical energy and, yet again, the whole is greater than the sum of its parts. That synergy, that mysterious and powerful force, permeated the Beatles' catalog and helped make them legends.

As true in life itself, we can do so much more good in the world with that same synergistic harmony working within mankind.

In this song, Paul sings a great interpretation of Right Knowledge. This is the culmination of the Eightfold Path and again I stress that this is the only road leading to eternal knowledge of all things. I ask only that you consider Right Knowledge and love in the grandest sense: talk about it, strive for it and meditate on it.

With goodwill for the entire cosmos, cultivate a limitless heart above, below, and all around, unobstructed without hostility or hate.

As the Beatles put it, "*....and in the end, the love you take is equal to the love you make.*"

ABOUT THE MUSIC

DJ Eddie: And what of this famous Fab Four farewell?

Buddha: The Beatles do not disappoint with this closing medley- masterpiece. It is an artwork tapestry of beautiful melody, vocal harmony, superb guitar and drum breaks all combined in an interwoven creativity, par excellence.

DJ Eddie: Zowie! Let me write that down!

Buddha: Paul starts things off with the stunningly gorgeous and melodic, yet beautifully simple, *Golden Slumbers*. From here, the band morphs into *Carry That Weight*, a driving segment with Ringo's drum work serving as the backdrop for three superb guitar interchanges between Paul, George and John.

Finally, we move to *The End*, a short little lyrical snippet citing "love" as the culminating and final message from the Beatles to literally billions of listeners worldwide from now until forever. How's *that* for the power of art?

THE TRIVIA

DJ Eddie: The Beatles had been disgruntled for a long time before, during and after the *Let It Be* film debacle. Over time, the group wisely agreed not to end things that way. The accounts are varied as to who exactly took the lead in resurrecting the band for one last album, but most sources largely credit this to Paul.

After discussing the idea of one more album amongst the band members, Paul rang up producer Martin and explained that they wanted to go back into the EMI studio and record like the old days, as a *real band* again and not as in the case of the *White Album's* collection of individual efforts. Martin was understandably a bit skeptical, but eventually agreed. He wanted to hear that synergistic magic again too.

Buddha: The result? The final Beatles' album, *Abbey Road*, became a legacy for inarguably the greatest pop band in history. But it took reconciliation, hard work, motivation, the right attitude and cooperation to get it home. Get it? Thanks to all your listeners, Eddie. I enjoyed talking with you and your audience.

DJ Eddie: Thank you, Buddha. Any closing thoughts or advice to our KOMM radio listeners?

Buddha: I can only offer the path to Right Knowledge to you all. But I cannot walk that path for you. Only you can walk the path. Stay persistent and try to become a better person with each day of your life.

The teaching is simple: Do what is right. Be pure. At the end of the way is freedom.

Thousands of candles can be lit from a single candle yet the life of the candle will not be shortened. Happiness never decreases by being shared. So stay in touch with DJ Eddie and me. Please visit: www.BuddahMeetsTheBeatles.com

Farewell for now, but not goodbye. And I do deeply love you all, *yeah, yeah, yeah! KOMM and DJ Eddie now off the air.*

How Many 5th Beatles Were There Anyway?

The "fifth (5th) Beatle" terminology and designation has been around for over half a century. Who really holds this title? The scorecard, as presented below, is admittedly totally subjective and enumerates up to an "18th Beatle," and there could be plausible arguments for even more. It does represent the first attempt known to mankind to actually draw attention to the many individuals who could actually be considered a "5th Beatle," or beyond. Order from chaos is generally a step in the right direction for a civilized society, so it is in that spirit that the list is presented here. In the end, each Beatlemaniac can freely decide for themselves!

The 5th Beatle was **Brian Epstein**

Originally a retail store owner, it could be argued that without Brian Epstein, the Beatles would have been regarded as just another Liverpool bar band. Brian discovered them, heard a sound he liked, believed in them, took the risks and eventually made it happen, *big-time*, to say the least! In the earliest days, Brian would buy Beatles' records himself at his own retail store so the records would appear to be sold out. Upon his death, the boys were visibly shaken. John in particular felt that the Beatles, already huge superstars, were in real trouble without him.

The 6th Beatle was **Sir George Martin**

More than just an ordinary session producer at EMI, Martin listened carefully to the audition tape brought to him by Mr. Epstein. Martin already knew that every other record company in London had turned down the Beatles, but he was willing to give the young lads a listen. Right off the bat, Martin enjoyed the boys' personalities and humor. In numerous documented accounts, Martin said that he heard something in their music that he liked. Further, he wasn't quite sure exactly what he liked, but he heard something that intrigued him. In the studio, he continued to add brilliance and innovation to the Beatles' productions, scored wonderfully rich orchestration and even ran interference on the Beatles' behalf with the EMI top brass.

The 7th Beatle was **Geoff Emerick**

Emericks' important book, *Here, There and Everywhere*, is a must read for Beatles' fans. The book offers excellent insights into the personalities of our four lads, Sir George Martin and the inner-workings of Beatles' recording sessions. Emerick was a major factor in capturing some very famous Beatle productions and is easily overlooked by many. His close miking techniques and creative studio approach is still highly regarded today. By the way, per EMI policies, Emerick received no printed credit or acknowledgement for his work until the back cover of *Abbey Road*, the Beatles' last official album!

The 8th Beatle was **Dave Dexter, Jr.**

Who, you ask? Fair question! With a formidable jazz background, and eventually rising to Director of Pop Music Operations for the U.S. label, Capitol, Dexter was in control of Beatles' releases and even the final mixes for the U.S. marketplace. Based in Hollywood, Dexter went as far as (without any Beatles' input) remixing Beatles' 45rpm singles for more radio "pop" or "sizzle" (i.e., usually adding more reverberation and compression to the U.K. original master tapes). As a result, in the U.S., all Beatles' fans heard only the "Dexterized" versions of all the Beatles' hits, whether over the radio or on vinyl records. Look carefully and you will read "Produced by Dave Dexter, Jr." on some U.S. vinyl platters on the Capitol label. (By the way, some of Dexter's re-mixes are superb!)

The 9th Beatle was **Stu Sutcliffe**

As a very talented paint artist, but phantom bass player, Stu filled a void for the very early Beatles stage act. No matter that he could hardly play a bass note, he was a great friend to his mates. Eventually, while gigging in Hamburg as a Beatle, Stu realized his limited musical abilities and decided to leave the group. This necessitated a new bass player for the stage band, enter McCartney, who up to this time was playing a regular guitar and a bit of piano. In fact, Paul said he felt "lumbered" by the bass when he took it over from Stu more or less by default. Paul certainly learned incredibly fast and became almost instantly a top-rated, world-class, electric bass player. Also worth mentioning, Stu's fiancé actually gave the Beatles their first "mop top" haircuts. Tragically, Stu died at a young age of a brain hemorrhage.

The 10th Beatle was **Pete Best**

Wildly popular in the earliest Beatles' days, Pete was, by most accounts, the ladies' "heart-throb" at the Cavern in Liverpool. A decent drummer by most accounts, George Martin was ill-impressed by Best at the Beatles' initial recording session at EMI. Martin brought in a session drummer (Andy White) to fill the void. Meanwhile, John and Paul asked Ringo to join the group. Best was let go, with specific reasons still unclear to this day. Lennon always said that Pete was a good drummer, but Ringo was a "better Beatle." History shows that Best has faired quite well under the circumstances. His various interviews reflect a man who came to terms with being tossed out of the Beatles, just before they broke through.

The 11th Beatle was **Murray the K**

DJ, Murray the K was instrumental in first bringing the Beatles' music to New York AM- radio. He broke the ice with Brian Epstein and started playing Beatles' records one after another giving the Fab Four their first serious airplay in America.

The 12th Beatle was **Dick James**

Brian Epstein was frantically trying to figure out the Beatles' publishing rights situation. The Beatlmania powder-keg was already beginning to explode skyward. No band in history ever made this much money from pop music this fast, at least not in the U.K. Dick James cut an early deal with Brian regarding the Beatles' music publishing.

The 13th Beatle was **Phil Spector**

By 1970, the Beatles, the world's most successful pop music group in history, was in total shambles. Recent recording sessions were so disjointed and lackadaisical that a commercial album was unilaterally scrapped by the band. John Lennon stepped in and with newly appointed manager, Allan Klein, a new producer, Phil Spector, was hired to salvage the former session tapes. Spector of course, already had huge success throughout the 1960s with his "wall of sound" producing acts like the Ronnettes and Righteous Brothers among many others. Spector proceeded to produce what became known as the *Let It Be* album. Although there is considerable disagreement among Beatles' aficionados, Spector's production magic created a reasonably saleable product and brought back to life Beatles' tunes that might have been otherwise lost.

The 14th Beatle was **Michael Jackson**

While recording with Paul on his 1983 solo album, *Pipes of Peace*, McCartney suggested to Michael that he get into the music publishing business. Just two years later, in 1985, Jackson took McCartney up on the idea and quietly outbid Paul for a 50% interest in all Beatles' compositions! Paul was not pleased. After Jackson's passing and the predictable, numerous legal battles, the bankruptcy court transferred Jackson's ownership portion of the music publishing rights from his estate to Sony/ATV Corporation.

The 15th Beatle was **Derek Taylor**

As the famed Beatles' press officer, Taylor had his hands full, especially in the troubled Apple Corps years in London. How do you deal with a constantly inquiring press in the midst of Beatle battles, wives, girlfriends, rumors, controversial and/or political statements by "the boys," such as John's "bigger than Jesus" misquote or Paul's "Yes, I've done LSD" remark. Make no mistake, being the press relations guy for the biggest pop band in history was no easy endeavor.

The 16th Beatle was **Neil Aspinall**

A very dear and close friend of the Beatles, Aspinall was truly a "right hand man" to the group. In later, post-Beatle years, Aspinall remained a confidant, office executive and close personal friend to Sir Paul.

The 17th Beatle was **Mal Evans**

Evans goes way back to the Beatles' earliest days, well before the mop-tops hit it big. Evans was the original "roadie," loading and unloading Beatle-gear in and out of a million smoky bars and clubs. He was truly one of the very few, from the inside, who saw the Beatles rise from literally nothing to worldwide fame. Part of his job description included driving the notorious old Beatle-van all over England in the middle of the night, while the boys slept pancake style to stay warm in the back. Evans even appears as a swimmer in the movie, "*Help!*," as he is continuously, and unsuccessfully, looking for the White Cliffs of Dover. Hilarious!

The 18th Beatle was **Norman Smith**

Norman Smith was the studio engineer for the early Beatles' recordings coming out of EMI. Working under George Martin, Smith was responsible for the studio procedures. He left the position assisting Martin in order to take on a higher level producer's role with another up and coming British band at the time, Pink Floyd!

Back Story

As iconic as the Beatles were musically, they may seem even more *significant than ever* when seen through the eyes of the Buddha. For starters, consider the group's synergy and how four young lads from the docks of a dingy, post-war hammered Liverpool, went on to transform pop music forever. This was Buddha's "harmony" working in quite a different way.

As their booming careers evolved, there were numerous challenges involving artistic and monetary struggles. Sadly, over the years there were many complex legal, contractual and monetary hassles to boot. And, among the four band mates there was a plethora of brotherly arguments, temporary break-ups and hurt feelings along the way. When the Beatles performed on the *Ed Sullivan Show* to the American TV audience, they were not the innocent, cute, mop-top guys most of the general public assumed they were.

Well before the Sullivan performance, the Beatles individually had experienced plenty of tragedy, including the passing of Paul's mother, Mary, and John's mother, Julia, both under very sad circumstances. There was also the passing of the earliest of "fifth Beatles," Stu Sutcliff. By the late 1960s, the death of their manager, Brian Epstein, only 32, caught the Fab Four by complete surprise, from which some may argue, they never fully recovered. Later, more sadness came with the early passings of Ringo's first wife, Maureen Cox, and Paul's soul mate, Linda Eastman-McCartney. And, of course, not a day goes by that a Beatles' devotee doesn't think about the premature deaths of John and George.

Also to consider, there were John's very difficult early years, growing up with his Aunt Mimi while his estranged father never really came back into his life. George had a strained relationship with his sister and Ringo had a near fatal illness as a young boy. And the list goes on.

So, as iconic as these four Beatles were, they too were never immune from *suffering*, and alleviating suffering is where Buddhist philosophy is rooted. That said, what's Buddhism all about anyway? And, what isn't it? This seems like a good time to briefly (*very* briefly) summarize what Buddhist philosophy is all about in the first place.

We start with the Four Noble Truths that simply say this:

1) All of life is *suffering*. This is not a pessimistic point of view, but a view of what life is, in reality. It's not as horrifying as it sounds. In time, as you delve deeper into Buddhism, you'll more clearly get the full meaning.

2) The cause of suffering is *desire*. "I want this" and "I want that," ad nauseam, and of course, it's never enough.

3) Suffering can end! If you can cease your desires (or "attachments"), you can end your suffering and achieve enlightenment.

4) The "Path" (aka, the *Eightfold Path*), is the way, and the only way, to get there (to attain enlightenment or Nirvana).

The heart of Buddhist thinking centers on simplicity, not complexity. To be living a Buddhist-principled life you need to merely follow (or at least aspire to follow as best you can) the Eightfold Path.

The Eightfold Path is comprised of:

1. Right Understanding. See things as they really are, not as you would like them to be and not with your own personal biases.

2. Right Thought. Approach everything in life with good intentions, using kindness and compassion.

3. Right Speech. Think before you talk! Major no-no's here would be using lies, slander, harsh words, gossip or cursing.

4. Right Action. Your everyday actions need to promote peace. Destructive behaviors of all types are not in the ballpark.

5. Right Livelihood. Do work that is helpful to others and spend your work hours being kind and peaceful toward others.

6. Right Effort. To live the right way, per this list, you've got to put in the correct effort. Your attitudes and thoughts need to be positive and harmonious.

7. Right Concentration. Cultivate your ability to focus your attentions. A basic cornerstone here is to be able to focus on your breathing as the road toward relaxation, deep thought and, ultimately, meditation and Zen.

8. Right Mindfulness. Exist in the present moment. Be mindful of your thoughts. Basically, stay in touch with you. The best way to do this is through the practice of meditation. But practice means practice. The more you do it, the better you get at it, sort of like figure skating!

The path above leads to Right Knowledge or Nirvana. Go for it!

A Quick Bio of the Buddha

Siddhartha Gautama Sakyamuni, known as "the Buddha," was born in 563 BC into royalty in an area that is now considered Nepal. His mother, Mahamaya, died eight days after he was born. His father, King Suddhodana, was afraid that Siddhartha would abandon the kingdom and kept him confined to the royal palace. At 20, Siddhartha's marriage was arranged to Princess Yasodhara.

At the age of 22, the previously confined Siddhartha finally discovered more about the outside world. He saw suffering everywhere. About this time, his son, Rahula, was born. By age 23 or 24, Siddhartha left his family, his position and the palace in search of worldly answers. This was a great sacrifice for him, but he felt compelled to travel and study the suffering in the world.

From his studies, Buddha learned about the interrelationships of different aspects of life and the actual causes of suffering. From the age of about 27 on, Buddha devoted his life to communicating his discoveries to the world so that others could find enlightenment. Buddha preached a middle path of behaviors that avoided extremes of either luxury or self-denial.

After many long years, he returned to his home as "the Buddha," which roughly translated means "the Awakened One." His wife Yashodara then joined him and her own life became one of devotion to the Buddhist path. The Buddha's teaching career lasted for 45 years until his death in 483 BC.

About the Author

Author, Ed Balian, at the entrance of the Cavern in Liverpool, England, famed site of regular Beatles' appearances during the early 1960s.

Edward Sarkis Balian has authored well over 450 works to date of various books, magazine articles, software, videos, professional papers, fine art photos and rock/pop/neo-classical/ballet music. In addition, as a fine art photographer and writer, he was Associate Editor of Shutterbug magazine for years before owning the magazine, PhotoWorld.

Together with 73 million American TV viewers, Ed was hopelessly and helplessly captivated by the Beatles at 8:03PM, Eastern Time, on February 9, 1964 when they took the stage on the Ed Sullivan Show. Almost before their first song of the evening ("All My Loving") was complete, Ed was already an avid collector of all things Beatles, including rare foreign import vinyl pressings, books, sheet music, documentaries, buttons, board games, guitars and the like. Ed personally saw the Beatles in concert in 1966 and still holds the ticket stub! Years ago, Ed was described by Beatles producer, George Martin, as "his greatest American Fan" in an autographed copy of Martin's book, All You Need is Ears.

Along the way, Ed attained the Ph.D. degree in Education from Wayne State University, Detroit---with the famous Motown Recording Studio virtually on the school campus! He has been a university professor and business consultant since 1974. Ed currently teaches at California State University, San Marcos.

As a back story, in 1968 Ed was part of the Detroit-based rock band, Andromeda, playing with the likes of many of the area's top local acts. By 1976, Ed teamed up with long time junior high school friend, Raymond George, and formed the George-Edwards Group, with sales of the duo's original music today in over 70 countries. Ed plays guitar, piano and bass and continues to write and record. The band's third album to date, Chapter III (released in 2014) is on the Drag City/Galactic Zoo (Chicago) label in vinyl, cd and iTunes formats. Their sound is often described by fans as a mix between the "folk-rock" of Simon & Garfunkel and "psych-rock," ala Pink Floyd.

Ed lives in San Diego and always loves to hear from others. He may be easily contacted through the website:

www.EdwardBalian.com

TOP: The author's ticket stub from August 13, 1966 Detroit concert (unretouched after almost 50 years, note price $5.50!)
BOTTOM: On stage at Olympia Stadium, Detroit, Michigan on September 6, 1964, during the first American tour.

Introductory Books on Buddhist Philosophy

These superb, easy-to-read and often humorous books offer basic introductions to Buddhist philosophy:

Awakening the Buddha Within by Lama Surya Das. Broadway Books, 1997. ISBN 0-553-06695-1

How to Become a Buddha in 5 Weeks by Giulio Cesare Giacobbe, Metro Books, 2005. ISBN 978-1-4351-2053-2

The Heart of the Buddha's Teaching by Thich Nhat Hanh. Parallax Press, 1998. ISBN 0-938077-81-3

201 Little Buddhist Reminders by Barbara Ann Kipfer. Ulysses Press, 2006. ISBN 1-56975-518-3

Worlds of Harmony by the Dalai Lama. Parallax Press, 1992. ISBN 978-1-888375-81-7

The Art of Happiness by the Dalai Lama. Riverhead Books, 1998. ISBN 1-57322-111-2

Buddhism for Dummies by Jonathan Landaw and Stephan Bodian. Wiley Publishing, 2003. ISBN 978-0-7645-5359-2

Essential Buddhism by Jacky Sach. Adams Media, 2006. ISBN 1-59869-129-5

The Everything Buddhism Book by Jacky Sach. Adams Media, 2003. ISBN 1-58062-884-2

The Religions of Man by Huston Smith. Harper & Row, 1958. ISBN 0-06- 080021-6